THE GOSPEL
OF GOD

THE GOSPEL
OF GOD

ANDERS NYGREN
Bishop of Lund

Translated by
L. J. TRINTERUD

SCM PRESS LTD
56 BLOOMSBURY STREET
LONDON

First published as
HERDABREV TILL LUNDS STIFT
Stockholm 1949

First published in Great Britain 1951

Printed in Great Britain by The Camelot Press Ltd.
London and Southampton

TRANSLATOR'S PREFACE

ANDERS NYGREN is one of Europe's most widely known and best-loved Churchmen. He was ordained to the ministry of the Gospel at the unusual age of twenty-one, and has served in the Church of Sweden a wide variety of assignments, from rural pastorate to bishop. Since the Lausanne Conference of 1927 he has represented his Church at nearly all ecumenical gatherings, and has become one of the leading figures in the ecumenical movement. As Bishop of Lund he will be host to the 1952 meeting of the World Council of Churches' Conference on Faith and Order. In 1947 Bishop Nygren became head of the Lutheran World Federation, and in that capacity has travelled widely in America, India, South Africa, Great Britain, and in numerous other countries.

It was through his writings that Bishop Nygren first became known in the wider circles of the Christian Church. For more than a quarter of a century he was professor of theology and ethics at the University of Lund. During this time he wrote a number of major works, several of which have been translated into German, Dutch, Japanese, English and French. His most definitive book, *Agape and Eros*, a study of the Christian doctrine of love, has been called one of the most important theological works written in this century. His vigorous attack on the Nazi Church policy, first published in 1934, was translated into English and Dutch, and early made him a leader in that long, hard struggle. Recently he has written the pilot volume (on Romans) for a new theological-exegetical commentary on the New Testament. This book also has appeared in an English translation.

It is the custom of the Church of Sweden that when a minister assumes the office of bishop he should send out to his diocese a pastoral letter. This present volume is a translation of Bishop Nygren's pastoral letter to the Diocese of Lund. A few of the more local and personal references have been omitted. The Biblical quotations have been translated from the modern Swedish translation used by Bishop Nygren.

L. J. T.

CONTENTS

I

THE PEACE OF GOD IN
CHRIST JESUS

*The peace of God which surpasses
all understanding, shall guard
your hearts and your thoughts,
in Christ Jesus.* PHIL. 4.7

THE PEACE of God is a boundless thing which does
not suffer itself to be caught in our small thoughts and
tiny categories. So, when it is said that God's peace
surpasses all understanding, that means that when we
seek to express by our understandings and our thoughts
that which God's peace is and implies, we shall always
fall far short. All too often this passage has been interpreted as though it meant that God's peace lies hidden
so deeply in the Christian's heart that even he himself is
usually unconscious of its presence, and that therefore
the Christian is far richer in peace than he himself can
understand. The Apostle, however, is speaking here of
something utterly different. He is speaking of peace
itself, and he is saying that peace is a thing so great, so
high, so overpowering, so divine, that it passes all
understanding. Even if we draw upon all our powers, and
all the resources of the understanding, as we ought to do,

9

even so, we shall learn that God's peace is greater and deeper than our thoughts about it, and that we shall never in any way be able to get to the bottom of it. Rather, we shall ever fall short of comprehending it.

At the same time there are two different ways of falling short. The one is fatal, the other is salutary.

The first way of falling short occurs when we begin with our own thoughts, and do not go beyond our own conceptions of what the peace of God signifies. For then we mislead ourselves, away from the truth, fail to get at the real issue and even misunderstand the reality which is involved in it. Just as little as anything else which pertains to God can be measured by human standards, so little can God's peace be handled thus without its being deformed and dissipated.

The second, the salutary way of falling short occurs when we allow ourselves to be led by God's revelation in the Scriptures, and regulate our thoughts according to its meaning. In the Scriptures much is said about the peace of God which has been given to us in Christ Jesus. But, when we penetrate deeply into it, and seek to fathom its significance, we come to learn ever anew that this reality which God gives 'surpasses all understanding.' It is altogether too great, in its unfathomable richness and depth, for us to capture within our thoughts and conceptions.

When the subject of God's peace is brought up for consideration it is easy for us to interpret it in accordance with what we otherwise know in ordinary human associations under the name 'peace.' We often use the word peace as a designation for a certain subjective state of mind. Peace is the opposite of anxiety and restlessness. It is a state of mind characterized by quiet and exalted repose. This definition of peace, taken over from everyday human life, is then applied to the peace of God. Thus, by 'God's peace' would be meant that quiet and harmonious state of mind in which that person finds himself who has his fortress in God. But, even if there may be some truth in such a description of God's peace, we may not rest content with it. By such human analogies we shall never reach to the essentials of the matter. These are but human ways of thinking which either lead us astray or allow us to rest in superficialities.

If we are to catch sight of the true significance of God's peace and penetrate deeper down into its mystery, we must forgo our own speculations and simply listen to what God's word has to say to us concerning it. Then we shall soon discover that God's peace looms up in a wholly different significance, and with wholly different dimensions, than what we had supposed. Now it is not merely a matter of an inward subjective state of mind, a feeling of harmony and quiet, but something infinitely greater. God's peace is an objective fact, a mighty reality, which embraces our entire existence. God's peace is that existence-form in which our lives as Christians, in all their totality, are set. We like to imagine that peace is a delicate thing, which we must lock up within ourselves, and protect, and hide in the depths of our hearts, so that it may not be lost or be evaporated. But in the Scriptures peace is spoken of in an utterly different way. There it is said that God's peace is a mighty power, which of itself can keep our hearts and our thoughts. God's peace is a mighty fortress, in which we are well defended and safe against all hostile powers of destruction. It is not we who are to protect peace, but rather it is peace which is to protect us.

If we have gotten our eyes well fixed on this greater perspective, and have come to realize that peace is a power, a divine *dynamis*, then we begin also to understand why the Lord Jesus, when He sent out His disciples, put the greeting of peace upon their lips. When they were commissioned to give the greeting of peace it was not to be merely a powerless wish that they were to express. Rather, by their Lord's commission they were to impart a gift of the utmost reality. Peace is a gift of Christ. It is conveyed through His disciples to that one who receives the greeting of peace. Henceforth, then, it may be said of him that 'peace rests upon him.' But, continued Jesus, if this gift of peace is rejected, 'so shall it return back upon yourselves' (Luke 10.6). Note the preposition 'upon' which is used here, when it is said that peace 'rests upon him.' This has something to say to us about the significance of peace. Just as God's wrath is a power which from above, from Heaven, comes down and like a terrible reality rests upon lost humanity (Rom. 1.18), so also is God's peace a power which in and through Christ comes down to us from above, and like a blessed reality rests upon redeemed humanity.

This leads us then a stage further. If the greeting of peace was to be the disciples' first word, it might seem that it was to be followed up by the proclamation of the essentials of the Gospel. That, however, would be an utter misunderstanding of the facts. The proclamation of

God's peace is not merely a beginning, or an introductory word, but it is just in itself the true and proper Gospel-proclamation. Jesus has sent His disciples to preach God's peace in His name, that and nothing else. In so far as that takes place, their commission is fulfilled.

The entire content of the Gospel is plumbed in the word of God's peace, because the entire content of the Gospel is Jesus Christ. To preach Him and to proclaim God's peace are one and the same. For it is He who has brought us God's peace. He is in His person and in His work so identical with God's peace, given to us, that the Apostle in Eph. 2.14 can say outright, 'He is our peace.' Christ Himself is our peace. Therefore also the Gospel concerning Him is called 'the gospel of peace' (Eph. 6.15).

Seen from one aspect all of Christ's work and mission is gathered up in this passage, 'He is our peace.' It was for this purpose that He came, that He should bring God's peace to a lost humanity. Even in the times of the Old Covenant it was known that this was to be His mission. Therefore He was called in prophecy, 'The prince of peace' (Isa. 9.6f.).

In agreement with this also, our Saviour's life from beginning to end was fixed upon that one objective—namely, to bring God's peace to us. This appears clearly in those decisive periods in His life as man, as well as in His suffering and death, and in His Resurrection. At the Saviour's birth the tidings of 'peace on earth' rang out. Therewith was the interpretation of His Incarnation given. For that meant that God's peace had come down to earth with Him, and that through Him it now rests upon us. And the same is true of his suffering and death. Why did He choose the way of degradation, suffering and the Cross? The answer is, 'punishment was laid upon him, that we might have peace' (Isa. 53.5). And, finally, the same is true of His Resurrection. There also peace stands at the centre. When the risen Lord revealed Himself to His disciples, time after time He summed up His message to them in the words, 'Peace be with you' (John 20.19, 21, 26). God's peace and Christ's Resurrection belong inseparably to one another, for in the Resurrection of Christ that new creation, which is characterized by God's peace, burst forth. So also the author of the Epistle to the Hebrews connects these two together when he says that it was the 'God of peace who brought again from the dead our Lord Jesus' (Heb. 13.20).

A clear picture of what God's peace means in the Christian life is given to us by the Apostle Paul in the fifth to the eighth chapters of his Epistle to the Romans. Earlier in the letter he has described, firstly, what human life is like now that it stands under God's wrath, and, secondly, how God through Christ revealed His righteousness, and how He gives that righteousness to each and every one who through faith belongs to Christ. It is this gift which Paul calls justification by faith. What then is the fruit of this God's act of justifying us? The answer is given to us by the Apostle in his fourth chapter. Like a summary title over the whole stand the words, 'Therefore, now that we have been justified by faith, we have peace with God through our Lord Jesus Christ' (Rom. 5.1). It would take too long to go through these chapters and show what they have to say about the new life in Christ and the peace of God which characterizes that life. It must be sufficient to point out but one noteworthy item. Just as the 'title' above this section closes with the words, 'through our Lord Jesus Christ,' so also each and every one of these chapters closes, one might almost say like a stereotype, with nearly the same words, 'through Jesus Christ, our Lord' (chs. 5 and 7), 'in Christ Jesus, our Lord' (chs. 6 and 8). Why this repetition? Why this stereotyped, recurring final note? Frequently the attempt has been made to conceive it as a sort of formalized concluding phrase which seeks less to give expression to any actual content than it does to give to the whole presentation a certain liturgical stateliness. Nothing could be more incorrect. There is in reality a very positive interest which leads the Apostle to close each of these chapters with the same words. When Paul says 'in Christ Jesus,' this is for him never merely a formula. In these words lie hidden the whole mystery of the Christian life. All that we as Christians have, we have solely and entirely 'in Christ Jesus.' 'He is our peace.' Without Him we should not have any peace of God. Without Him we would yet stand continually under the wrath of God. But now God has come to us in Christ Jesus and has given us His love, His righteousness, His peace. In Christ God has revealed and demonstrated to us that He has thoughts of peace and not destruction, in order to give to us a future and a hope (Jer. 29.11).

Jesus said to His disciples: 'My peace I give unto you; I do not give unto you as the world gives' (John 14.27). That peace of God which we have in Christ Jesus has nothing in common with that which in the world goes under the name of peace. In the world the old æon holds sway. In the kingdom of Christ God's peace holds sway. In the world distress dominates, but Christ has overcome the world. He has come forth from God and has brought peace to this our world, so that we, right in the midst of our ordinary, daily life, may live protected by the peace of God in Christ Jesus: in the midst of this world partakers of the life of the world to come.

II

WE ARE HERALDS

FROM TIME to time a word, or an expression, which strikes us becomes, quite involuntarily, etched on our hearts, and assumes the significance of a direct personal summons. If we are observant, we shall beyond doubt discover a good many such expressions. Here I wish to mention only one expression which has come to have such a significance for me. It is found in our Church's service book, one which occurs in almost exactly the same formulation in several different places: in the ordination service for a minister, in the installation service for a pastor, and in the ordination service for a bishop. When he who is to be ordained or installed stands there before the altar of the Lord to receive his ministry, the assistants gathered about the altar-rail direct to him a number of passages from the Scriptures. The object of this reading of Scripture is to be found in the section of the service which immediately precedes it. In the ordination service for a minister it reads, 'To the end that you with us, and we with you, may rightly consider the sacredness of this call, let us now hear God's word of promise and of admonition.' At the ordination of a bishop, or at the installation of a pastor, it is said, 'To the end that you, dear brother, with us, and we with you, may rightly consider the sacredness of your call, we shall now hear God's word of promise and of admonition.'

When I try to recall to memory that time when this expression first struck my ears and etched itself upon my heart, I am carried far back to the earliest years of childhood, to an ordination service in the Cathedral of Gothenberg before the turn of the century. The words were instinct with a unique spirit which no one who has been caught by them can ever forget. Here the unseen became a tangible reality in a unique manner, the spiritual became simple and irresistible fact. Here one could almost grasp palpably what sacredness is, 'the sacredness of this call.' Later, these words became a direct personal confrontation for me when, barely twenty-one years old, I was ordained to the ministry in that same Cathedral in Gothenberg. When the various passages of Scripture, each in turn, were read out by the assistants, their very sequence served to make clear that the office of the ministry is not a thing which we have at our disposal but rather a thing which is given to us and for which we must make an accounting. It is something important and responsible, concerning which we, led by that divine word, must bethink ourselves, 'You with us, and we with you.'

This expression has since followed me through the years, as I have served as an assistant at more than fifty ordination services. They have followed me even until, with a peculiar meaning, they again met me in a personal confrontation before the altar in the Cathedral at Uppsala, when I received ordination to this my present office.

Who then are *we*, who are summoned to consider with one another the sacredness of our call?

The first answer which must be given to this question sets us in the midst of the hosts of all the Christian faithful. In actual fact there is no difference between us ministers and other Christians. Whatever is true of us, is true of all. Or, better said, only that which is true of all Christians, is true also of us. Of all Christians, without exception, is the word true, 'Ye are a royal priesthood, a holy people, a peculiar people, in order that ye might preach the wondrous works of him who has called you out of darkness into his marvellous light' (I Pet. 2.9). Of all the members of Christ is it said that they are priests. There reigns the 'universal priesthood.' All have a part in that deed which God wrought in Christ. They are all those who, like living stones built upon Christ who is Himself 'the living stone,' are said to be built up into a spiritual house and thereby ordained to be 'a holy priesthood, which shall bring forth spiritual sacrifices, which through Jesus Christ are well-pleasing to God' (I Pet. 2.4f.). Here no differences are struck. One and the same thing is true of all Christians. The essential, the highest, the all-decisive they have in common in Christ. They are all members in one and the same body (Rom. 12.4f.; I Cor. 12.12ff.). They are all 'God's beloved, called, and holy' (Rom. 1.7). When we now set about to reflect upon the minister's call and task, it is of importance that it first be said, with all emphasis, that all Christians in the deepest and innermost sense have one and the same call and election of God.

But as soon as that has been said, the question recurs

with new significance: Who are *we* who are being summoned together in order to consider the sacredness of our call? What is that task which has been entrusted to us as ministers in Christ's Church? The very statement that we all as Christians are members of one and the same body, in Christ, carries with it an indication that there is a special task which has been given to us. 'For just as we, in one and the same body, have many members, but all the members have not the same functions, so also we, even though many, constitute one single body in Christ, but we are distinct members for the purpose of mutual service. And we have different gifts according to the grace which has been given to us' (Rom. 12.4ff.).

All members have not the same function. That is in the very nature of the matter. The body is indeed one, but its members are many, differing from one another in structure and in function. This very dissimilarity is here of decisive significance. Only in the unison of all the different members in their differing functions can the body as a whole live its complete life. This the Apostle applies to Christ and His congregation, 'Now are ye Christ's body and his members, each and every one in his measure' (I Cor. 12.27). Thereafter follows an exposition of how God has ordained in the congregation various offices and has given diverse gifts, all of which are to be used in the service of the whole.

All members have not the same function. What then is that function which is the *special* task that has been assigned to us who have been called to be ministers in the congregation of Christ? What are we? That question can perhaps be most simply answered with a passage taken from the account of the call of Isaiah (Isa. 6.8). We are those who have known the word of the Lord addressed to us, 'Whom shall I send, and who will be our heralds?' and who have answered that question with, 'Lo, here am I, send me.' *Heralds*—that is the decisive word which designates the minister's *special* call and task. The Lord has a Gospel which He will have brought to His congregation and to the world. Therefore He seeks heralds, and it is as such that He wills to use ministers.

We are heralds—that and nothing else. The Gospel which we have received from God constitutes our whole being as ministers. All that which otherwise can be said of our task as ministers is secondary to this, and must be traceable back to the fact that we are heralds, and that God has a Gospel which He will have proclaimed through us. It is the more important to make this fact itself utterly clear, because at various times, and in various parts of Christendom, a very different interpretation of that which is essential in the minister's call has prevailed.

Let us cite a few examples. Very early an interpretation pushed its way into the Church according to which the primary function of the ministry ought to be that of a sacrificing priesthood, men who by virtue of their ordination were in a position to present an efficacious and purifying sacrifice. Again, men have wanted to see in the clergy *mystagogues*, who by their *gnosis*, by their familiarity with the higher world and its secrets were able to lead souls on to the right way to heaven. Or, again, ministers were *instructors*, who drew their teachings out of the treasures of the divine revelation, and whose principal task was to watch over the purity of doctrine. Or the minister has been understood as being a moral nurturer, or trainer, who through his directions and his corrections induced men to lead a moral life. Or the minister was looked upon as the *religious virtuoso*, who among other things can impart something of 'the power of his God-consciousness.' Or he might be seen as a *witness*, who can recount something of his own subjective religious experiences and thereby arouse similar experiences in others. More recently the minister has often been regarded by some as a *propagandist*, whose primary task was that of securing for the Christian world-view, or the Christian ethic, a hearing in contemporary affairs either against or alongside of other ideologies, other world-views, or other ways of life. Or it has been asserted that the minister's primary task is that of being a *spiritual guide*, and to include with that the conception of someone who, with good psychological and therapeutic insight, can take charge of people who have spiritual conflicts, and contribute to their harmonious restitution.

The list of specimens is comprehensive, and yet these are only some examples. But of all these interpretations it must be said, either that they are false, or, that at any rate they are decidedly superficial and in no way arrive at that which is essential in the minister's task. As regards the first interpretation, that of a sacrificing priesthood, it is wholly false. In other religions there is a place for sacrificing priests; indeed, there the offering of sacrifices is central in the priest's duties. But in the congregation of Christ there is no longer any place for such. The Gospel signifies the great revolution in the religious world. The sacrifice which reconciles us to God is not our act, but

God's. 'It was God who in Christ reconciled the world to himself' (II Cor. 5.19). When Christ delivered Himself up He presented that sacrifice which replaced and made antiquated the old sacrificial order. It is with this which the Epistle to the Hebrews deals explicitly. 'When he says "a new covenant," he has thereby made it known that the previous one is antiquated' (Heb. 8.13). The entire sacrificial system of the old covenant is in and through Christ made antiquated. Christ is the new covenant's only high-priest, the offering brought by Him is the sole, but also the eternally efficacious, sacrifice. Until the time of Christ there was a place for the priest's continually repeated sacrifices, and for the high-priest's atoning sacrifice. But with Christ the time of the high-priest has come to an end. For when Christ offered Himself He did it 'once for all' (Heb. 7.27, 9.28). Here there is no place for a new offering. Here there is no longer any place for a sacrificing priesthood.

Likewise it would be false to comprehend the minister as a religious virtuoso or as the spokesman for a Christian ideology. The Christian faith is not a psychological capacity which must be cultivated and improved. And the Gospel is not an ideology, nor some world-view or way of living. It is rather a living and concrete message, a Gospel. Neither is the minister's major task that of propounding that religious philosophy which is supposedly acknowledged by the congregation. His task is just that of bringing to the congregation this concrete message, the Gospel.

And even if one may with full right speak of the minister's task as teacher, nurturer, witness, and spiritual guide, this may be done aright only if one does it in the realization that his primary task is that of proclaiming a divine Gospel. Let me illustrate this from the task of a spiritual guide.

Certainly the minister must be a spiritual guide. Altogether too often this task has fallen into the background. But this does not mean that the minister should have the function of caring for the mental hygiene of his congregation through the use of certain general principles. Only a secularized view would make the minister parallel to the psychotherapist in the cure of souls. The Christian cure of souls is not something else alongside of the Gospel but just the Gospel applied to the individual, a Gospel for that person. That the cure of souls in recent times has fallen so much by the wayside is quite clearly connected with the dwindling consciousness of the fact that the Gospel is a personal message. For where that consciousness is clear and living, and where the auditor also hears the preached word as a message directed to him personally, there arises in him the need of having his personal standing to that message clear. In other words, he comes to that situation which the Christian cure of souls presupposes.

The specific task of the Christian cure of souls is never the resolution of spiritual and mental conflicts as such. Rather the Christian cure of souls has to do with man as he is confronted by the divine Gospel. To be sure, it is a fact that nearly all spiritual and mental conflicts, in one way or another, have something to do with man's relationship to God. Therefore they do, it is true, appear in a new light when brought into confrontation with the Gospel. Accordingly, in the cure of souls none of these conflicts

24

may be looked upon as foreign, or irrelevant. Nevertheless, it is a most serious error to conduct the cure of souls purely from the standpoint of these conflicts themselves, or to see in the cure of souls nothing more than a means for resolving these conflicts. Such an attitude, utterly secularized, has indeed so far succeeded in forcing its way into theology, and into the Church, that even there a conception of the Church's task in the cure of souls has become accepted according to which the Christian cure of souls would be meaningful only in so far as it got these psychological conflicts resolved. In opposition to this we must by all means arrive at an evangelical concept of the cure of souls, in which the cure of souls primarily means the personal application of the Gospel.

We are heralds. What Gospel are we then sent out to proclaim? The Christian Gospel, of course. Very often the issue is so stated as though our task were that of preaching 'Christianity.' In and of itself, to be sure, the answer even in the latter formulation is wholly correct. Even so, it carries with it grave risks. When we say that it is our task to preach 'Christianity,' that can easily give rise to the notion that it should be our task to proclaim an objective doctrine, a Christian system of thought. It would be better, therefore, to express it thus: there is a Gospel which we are to proclaim. The word 'Gospel' declares plainly what is here involved. For, *euangelion* means merely 'news,' 'good news,' 'joyful news.' We ministers ought never to forget the prophet's words, 'How beautiful are the footsteps of the herald of gladness, as he comes over the mountain, to proclaim peace and bring good news, and proclaim salvation' (Isa. 52.7).

That is exactly our position, and our task, if we understand it aright. We are heralds, heralds of gladness. We have received overwhelming, joyful news to proclaim to the world. This is central in all our diverse tasks, and that which, in the final analysis, makes them all come together into one single task. We have a teaching task, a nurturing task, the task of the cure of souls, but these we have solely as the consequence of the fact that we have been sent out as heralds to tell some great news which has taken place in our world, something which has to do with each and every one.

We are heralds, we are ambassadors (II Cor. 5.20)—that is the 'sacredness of our call,' and likewise that which puts us in our proper place. Apart from his message, the herald is nothing in particular. It is not upon him and his person that the importance lies, but upon the message which he has to proclaim. Upon the message everything is concentrated. It is from this that our call receives its sacredness. All other interpretations of the minister and his task come, to a greater or a lesser degree, to lay the stress upon the minister himself, upon his capacities, upon his qualifications, upon his importance. The sacrificing priest *is* something. Through his priestly character he has the situation in hand. He *can* do something which others cannot. He is in possession of a special power, the power to propitiate by means of the sacrifice which he makes. It is the same with the *mystagogue*. He is the wise man. By the power of his *gnosis* he raises himself above the others. Also the religious witness in a certain degree places himself in the centre, in so far as his message is based upon a witness to his own religious experiences. Beyond all others, the minister understood as the religious virtuoso occupies the centre of the stage. His is the task of imparting to his fellow men something of his spiritual powers.

For us as ministers in the Church of Christ God has so ordered it that *we* do not need to stand in the centre. It is not from out of ourselves that we are to draw in our proclamation. No power is laid in our hands. No special qualifications render us equipped as spiritual leaders. The one thing which has been given to us is the Gospel, but a Gospel of which it can be said, in that word's truest meaning, that power dwells within it. 'God's word is living and powerful, and sharper than any two-edged sword, and penetrates through, so that it separates soul and spirit, marrow and bone; and it is a judge of the intents and thoughts of the heart' (Heb. 4.12). That word we have been commissioned to proclaim. 'The Gospel is a power of God unto salvation for each and everyone who believes' (Rom. 1.16). This is the Gospel we are to give out. The power does not come from us, rather it lies within the Gospel itself. We are but those who deliver it. We are heralds. That is the sacredness of our call.

III

THE GOSPEL
CONCERNING CHRIST

THAT WHICH gives our work as ministers content and
meaning is the Gospel, that, and only that. We are but
messengers, the passing bearers of that Gospel. Let us
therefore now turn our attention away from ourselves,
the heralds who so soon pass away, to the message itself.
What is the content of this message?

We have already emphasized the utter difference
between an objective, timeless doctrine and a concrete
message. Even so, it is well that here at the very beginning
we pause long enough to bring out as clearly as possible
the unique character of the Gospel message. When it is
said that the Gospel is a message addressed to us, all too
often we merely accept this word 'message' without
considering seriously what it is to which this word seeks
to give expression. For simple and natural reasons, our
whole attitude toward the Gospel is such that we find it
very difficult to grasp the thought expressed in the word
'message' when it is used of the Gospel. If word comes
to me that a friend, who I feared had been killed in a
traffic accident, has been rescued, I have no difficulty in
interpreting that word as a message. To be sure, seen
from one side it is an objective and timeless truth which

is thereby conveyed to me. But for me this same truth has the significance of a personal message. It ought to be the same with the Gospel. Yet here we find it much harder to grasp the concept of a real message. The Gospel has been preached generation after generation, from century to century. It is an old and familiar truth, which we find it hard to apprehend as a new message. The message has petrified, and has become an objective teaching, about which we can ascertain: Yes, that's the way it is—and then go on our way. When the minister preaches the word of God, it all too easily happens that for both him and his hearers it is a matter of annotating the text and setting forth certain religious truths, rather than that of a true message. But if one does not hear the Gospel as a message, it is no longer the Gospel which he hears. For gospel means just 'good news,' a message of joy.

Nothing is more important than that we hear the Gospel as a message directed to us. But just exactly what is meant by saying that the Gospel comes as a message? What is a message? Let me illustrate by an example from another area.

During the late world war various countries were invaded by usurping powers. The yoke of occupation rested heavily upon these countries. Although Sweden did avoid that fate, still even we had an intimate perception of the fearfulness of such an occupation. Not the least reason for this was the fact that our neighbours, Denmark and Norway, were among the occupied countries. But, then one day in May, 1945, came the message, 'Denmark is free!' 'Norway is free!' When this news went out over these two countries it was indeed a message, in the truest meaning of that word. Even for us in Sweden it came as a message, since our brethren's hard fate had come so close to us that we had come to look upon it as our own. Those who experienced those days, and that sensation of jubilation which gripped all because of that message, have therein an illustration of what a message, an overwhelming story of good news, joyful news, really is.

In order to get an even clearer idea of what is meant by a message, let us pause for a moment and analyse further this situation. The first thing to note is that a message involves a telling or a story of something which has happened. But mere narration is still not the same thing as a message. When several hundred years from now someone reads in a history an account of the freeing of these two occupied countries, the story will no longer have the character of a message. It will then be merely the correct and dull repetition of an objective, historical fact. How can that repetition say that when this event first occurred the story of it came as news, as a message? To be sure, that does not mean that the objectivity of the fact which made the news would play no role when it was read about in later history. On the contrary, the presupposition of any news or message is that something has really happened. Nevertheless there is more to it than that. In addition, that which is told must be of vital importance to those who are to hear it. A power stronger than the occupying powers has come, and has deprived them of their dominion. That is the objective thing which has taken place. But—and this is the other no less important side of the matter—at the same time a stupendous transformation of each individual's subjective situation has taken place. They who once had been driven under-ground by fear of the occupying powers may now venture forth again. The law, which had been set aside, has now been restored. The period of lawlessness and arbitrary rule is gone. One can breathe again, and begin to live.

That example gives us a good idea of what is meant by a message. It shows us how an objective and a subjective element here work together, and how both of these two elements constitute a message only when inseparably conjoined. For if we are to be able to speak of a message, there must first of all be at hand some objective fact about which the message tells. Had that objective fact not taken place, had not a more mighty power come and struck down the oppressor, things would have remained as they had been. Violence, lawlessness, and fear would have continued to hold sway. But, and here we come to the other aspect of the matter, so long as the news of that which had taken place had not reached the individual who lay in prison or who was in hiding, it was as if nothing had happened. Life still had its old appearance, and tyranny still had its grip upon men. Only when both of these two things, which we called the objective and the subjective elements, are present and concurring, only when victory was objectively won and the news of it was spread over the land, only then did the chains fall off, the fear disappear, and men could return to decent human living. The objective change which took place brought with it a subjective change as well—or one might better say, it brought with it an objective change in the in-dividual's situation. He can say: the freeing of my land has also restored to me my personal freedom.

Why have we given this example? In order to give a clear and concrete idea of what is meant by a message, and especially, in order to illustrate the content of the Christian message. For this purpose the example is, moreover, unusually apt. It does not merely present some vague sort of analogy to the Christian message. Rather there is a real correspondence here.

Our human life is by nature a life under alien powers of violence. How this has come to be is a matter which we cannot in detail either comprehend or explain. No one has ever been able to give a satisfactory theoretical explanation of 'the problem of evil.' But, that our situation is under these alien powers is a patent fact. In this agree both the Biblical testimony and all human experience. In the Scriptures these powers of evil go under the name of Sin and Death. It is of set purpose that these names are here capitalized. In this way their character as powers which dominate our life is expressed. This is a different view from that which we are accustomed to assume. When we speak of death, we usually think of an event, or a situation which brings to an end our earthly life, cuts the cord of life, snuffs out the flame of life. This also presupposes that we for a certain time find outselves in that situation which is called 'life,' and which by its very nature is the opposite of death. It presupposes that this life is at a certain point taken from us, and that we thereupon revert to death. But when, for example, the Apostle Paul speaks of Death he does so with a wholly different meaning. Death is not just something which takes over after our earthly life. Death is that power which dominates this our present life. The very nature of this existence which we call life is what the Apostle calls Death. This view comes to a like expression in that old medieval song which was taken up by Luther, 'In the midst of life we are surrounded by death,' or, as it reads in our Swedish version, 'We on earth live here prisoners under death.' We live here on earth, yes. Certainly we live, but the question is: just how is that life constituted, and under which ruler does it stand? The answer must be: it is a life captive under Death, from beginning to end marked by Death.

In time past this Christian concept of the natural human life has often met with contradiction. Men have asserted that there is no reason for taking such a 'dark' and 'pessimistic' view of human life. How much of greatness and of value is there not to be found in the science, the art, and the social institutions of human culture! Should all this in its totality be devoid of worth? This line of reasoning, however, rests upon a complete misunderstanding of the Christian view. In the very nature of things there is no thought of proclaiming in the name of the Christian faith such a negative view of human culture. No, human culture is something great and valuable, the fruit of the use and cultivation of those gifts with which the Creator has endowed us. That which is here under discussion is rather something which penetrates far deeper down. Of all human life, even of the most exalted, it is true that it stands under the law of Death. Here it is not a matter of deprecating something, but quite simply a matter of seeing under what conditions human life in its totality, from its lowest to its highest forms, is placed.

In that regard we to-day stand in a somewhat different situation from that which we did previously. Our generation, which has undergone two world wars, and which now lives under the shadow of the fear of a third, has learned a realism wholly foreign to earlier generations. But therewith it has also received wholly new possibilities for understanding the realism of the Biblical view that human life is placed under the dominion of Death. If we did not know anything of that before, we have certainly seen it in recent years as men did all within their power to rend and destroy themselves. Men literally hurled down death upon each other. To be sure, there are many in our day who see nothing and perceive nothing. But one must be very blind indeed if he lives right in the midst of this most recent phase of human history, and yet has not in some way come up against that to which the Christian view of human life witnesses—namely, that man's life is under the dominion of Death.

The perplexity which now dominates the world is certainly to all a patent fact. One surely does not need to assume any special Christian viewpoint in order to see so patent a fact. Perplexity is a fact which is apparent for one and all who have eyes to see. But the interpretation of that fact which is patent to all will, to be sure, vary according as one either does, or does not, look at it with Christian eyes. For the Christian it is clear that the perplexity which holds sway in the world is not just something accidental, due to unfortunate circumstances, faulty organization, or the wickedness of individual men. All such interpretations are superficial. The real and deepest ground of the tragedy of human life lies in the fact that God's own world has become alienated from Him. It is a world aloof, and rebellious against Him. Therefore it lies under the evil powers of Sin and Death. For a humanity which turns its back upon God is working out its own destruction (cf. Rom. 1.21–32). In any event, so much should be clear, that it is of things most actual and real that the Christian faith speaks when it says that this life is placed under the domination of Death.

Something comparable to what has been said of Death as a power over human life is true also of Sin as a power. Here again, we have accustomed ourselves to a serious misinterpretation. We minimize and deprecate the term sin in a moralistic direction, as though it were merely a matter of individual wrong acts. If we go to the New Testament, we get another view entirely of the significance of Sin. Sin is not, as we like to imagine, merely certain moralistic errors of which we are guilty. Sin is a mighty power, which holds us and our entire race in its grip. When a man gives himself over to Sin, he does it willingly, thinking that he is lord over his acts. Another time he can determine to do the good instead. Here the Scriptures have an altogether different view. They condemn such thoughts as mere illusions. 'He who commits sin, he is the slave of sin.' It is not man who is lord over sin, but sin which is lord over him. Sin is a power which holds him as a vassal. By nature we stand together with our whole race under that terrible, alien domination. Only a most superficial examination can produce the conclusion that man is sovereign in this regard, and that he has the good or the evil in his own power of choice. It is just as if someone should say to a person in an occupied country, 'It's entirely up to you as to whether you are to live in freedom or to be under an alien power.' To be sure, much does depend upon our choice. When we act contrary to God's will, we cannot hide ourselves and say, 'I had no other choice. I was compelled, against my will.' On the contrary, when Sin masters a man it does so by conquering his will. Then he does sin willingly and readily. However, one thing does not depend upon our choice—namely, whether or not we shall be sinners. It was not we who chose that we should be members of our sinful race. We were born in that association. No one enquired after our desires or our approval. An inexorable necessity unites the whole human race, in Sin.

The Apostle Paul, in his Epistle to the Romans, gives special attention to these powers of destruction which have chained all of human life. In addition to the two powers already mentioned, Death and Sin, he names two more, the Wrath of God, and the Law. In order not to complicate unduly this presentation, we shall omit here any discussion of these latter two powers. Enough has been said about Sin and Death to make clear the meaning of the Biblical conviction that human life is under the domination of alien powers.

Strictly speaking, of course, a discussion of the powers of destruction is no part of the Gospel. That our lives are enslaved under hostile powers is not a message of good news. It is a hard reality which we all know only too well by experience. Yet one often runs on to the notion that all this talk about the powers of destruction which dominate human life ought really to be understood as being no more than some sort of a dark background which is needed merely to make the Gospel stand out in fairer, brighter colour. In other words, this talk about Sin and Death is but an artificial aid, or prop, invented for a purpose. Nothing could be more false than such a notion. The power of Sin and Death is plain, unavoidable reality. It is a fact in human life with which a man must try to come to terms—and that regardless of whether or not he believes in the Christian Gospel. He who rejects the Gospel may use other names for this reality, and he would, of course, interpret it in another way. But the fact which is indicated by the Christian name remains there all the while, even for the unbeliever.

Even though, then, this word about the powers of destruction, the domination of Sin and Death over human life, is no part of the Gospel itself, and is actually its direct opposite, nevertheless it is real, and because it is real it has a true function. It shows us the actual situation into which the Gospel comes. This is our real predicament, this is the lot which is inseparable from the natural human life.

To us who live in this land occupied by Sin and Death there now peals forth the Gospel of God: God has intervened in Christ for our deliverance. 'The people who wander in darkness shall see a great light; yes, over those who dwell in the land of the shadow of death shall a light shine clearly. You shall break asunder the yoke of their burdens, the scourge of their guilt, the rod of their oppressor' (Isa. 9.2, 4). The Gospel is realistic, it takes our existence as it really is. It confesses that the powers of destruction do dominate and exercise their régime of force over our life. But at the same time it speaks of a power which is greater than theirs. God's power is stronger than all the powers of destruction. Jesus said, 'When a strong man, fully armed, keeps guard over his estate, then are his possessions secure. But if someone who is stronger than he attacks him and overcomes him, then the stronger one takes from him all his weapons upon which he relied, and plunders him' (Luke 11.21f.). It was just this which happened when God sent Christ into the world. There the powers of destruction were ruling, and none could dispute their dominion. But, then came Christ as the stronger one who attacked and over-came the strong man, and took from him his spoil. In agreement with the Old Testament prophets, Jesus Himself also interprets His work thus, that He came to bring 'freedom to the prisoners' (Luke 4.18), freedom from the domination of the powers of destruction.

In Christ God has given our race a new beginning. Though we, by belonging to the old man whose head is Adam, are the children of death, nevertheless, God has now through Christ created for Himself a new humanity for which Christ is the head, and through Him we now participate in life's new aeon. 'For since death came through one man, so also through one man came the resurrection of the dead. And as in Adam all die, so also shall all be made alive in Christ' (I Cor. 15.21f.). He who believes in Christ is, through belonging to Him, free from all the powers of destruction. He is free from God's wrath, not through his own act, but through Christ's atoning. He is free from Sin, not in the sense that he is sinless in a moralistic meaning, but in the sense that Sin is no longer his master. He stands under another Lord, Jesus Christ. And in the same sense he is free from the Law and free from Death. The great about-face from Sin to Righteousness, from Law to Grace, from Death to Life, took place when God sent Christ into this lost world and when Christ gave Himself for us. This is that great objective thing which has taken place.

Now it has often been argued that if this really has happened, if the atonement has occurred once for all, if deliverance from the powers of destruction has been won, then nothing more is needed. The situation of the human race has been changed, and we as members of that race are participants in that change. Such a notion is, however, utterly false. To be sure, salvation is from beginning to end an objective fact, which God has brought about through Jesus Christ. But it is not an objective drama in the sense that it takes place without us. What would it be like, if that man who went 'underground' never came to know that his land had become free, or if he never dared to place any confidence in the news of freedom? Certainly that would not alter the fact that his country had been freed. But he himself would have no part in that freedom. He would have to continue to conceal himself. He would forever live in his old fear, and remain the slave of those masters who had in reality lost their power and authority over him. This is the reason that God's word meets us not merely as theoretical information, or a universally valid doctrine, but rather as a message, that is to say, as a word directed personally to him who hears it, appealing to his faith. God has acted through Christ. If I believe, then I have the deliverance.

If I do not believe, then I do not have it. It simply does not exist for me.

God's act in Christ was a mighty act directed against the powers which hold our lives in thraldom. God begins and completes this His mighty act for our salvation when He has the Gospel, which is simply the news of this His act in Christ, proclaimed among us. From this standpoint we can also understand the Apostle Paul when he characterizes the Gospel as 'God's power unto salvation for each and every one who believes' (Rom. 1.16). When the Gospel is here described as a power, this word ought to be understood in its literal meaning. The Gospel is a word, a message. But it is not a powerless word. It is not merely an account of a mighty act which God once performed, but which now belongs only to the past. It is a word which is 'living and powerful.' It lays hold with power on our existence and makes that which once took place through Christ living and powerful in our present life—unto salvation and liberation from those powers of destruction.

Just as the significance of Sin is often slighted, and Sin is given a trivial moralistic interpretation, so also the significance of salvation is often slighted, as though it were merely a matter of a psychological or moral straightening out of the difficulties of our lives. This distorts and shrivels the Gospel. We must by all means learn that the Gospel has not only psychological, but also cosmic dimensions. The Gospel is a power which conquers other opposing powers and frees us from their domination.

The Gospel is the message of 'the revelation of our Saviour, Jesus Christ,' and how He 'annihilated the power of death, and brought life and immortality to light' (II Tim. 1.10). He who believes on Him shall *live* (Rom. 1.17)—that is to say, he may enter into that new æon which has come through Christ, the æon of life. His life no longer stands under the domination of Death, but 'he has passed from death to life' (John 5.24). He has been fitted into a new context, in which Sin and Death do not rule, but Righteousness and Life. For 'if anyone is in Christ, he is a new creation. The old has passed away, behold something new has come' (II Cor. 5.17). The old bondage to this world's powers of destruction has passed away. Something totally new has come—namely, participation in Christ's life, the resurrection life, the life of the coming world. This life is already being given, in an initial way, to him who believes on Christ, in order that it may later be completed in glory.

It is for this purpose that this Gospel shall sound forth, that this message of freedom shall be proclaimed everywhere and never be silenced—namely, that the Church of Christ has been established among us. It is for this reason that churches lie spread all the world around. And it is for this reason that divine service is held every Sunday, year after year, century after century. That this Gospel shall be proclaimed is also the reason that we ministers have been ordained. Our task is none other than that of being messengers who bring the message of Christ and of that victory over the powers of destruction which God has given us through Him. Let us not, however, so misunderstand the word that we are *only* messengers, as to think that being a messenger is something trivial. We are involved in a mighty conflict, in which the

Gospel and the powers of destruction contend for
dominion over human life. To be sure, the Word is our
only weapon—we are nothing other than messengers, we
have *only* the Word. But, it is no powerless word. It is
rather a word in which power dwells. The message which
God gives us to present is the message of God's act, but
the message itself is likewise an act of God. Each time
this message is proclaimed, it means that God begins
and completes His deed in us. When the Gospel comes
upon the scene, God then and there frees man from the
dominion of the powers of destruction, and makes him a
member of that new humanity whose Lord and Head is
Christ.

In the foregoing we have discussed four concepts
which belong inseparably together: messengers, message
(Gospel), power, deed. To these we can now add a fifth,
reality. Actually, this fifth concept has been involved all
the while, and has formed the background for all that has
been said. But for the sake of clarity it is necessary now
at the last to bring it out and place it in the foreground.

It is a common—but none the less false and untenable
—supposition that all that which religion is 'has its seat
in the feelings,' and that religion, therefore, in the final
analysis has nothing to do with ultimate reality. Whatever such a notion may be worth in other contexts, it
nowhere fits into the Christian faith. From beginning to
end the Gospel lays claim to being founded upon reality.
The Christian faith speaks of our human situation as it
truly is, and that message upon which faith rests is a
message about such things as really happen in this our
world. He who is a complete stranger to the Christian

faith must quite naturally think that all this talk of Sin and Death sounds a bit 'mythological'—and that especially when it is emphasized that these are powers which dominate human life. Is there actually something real about all this? Yet, if this man will but look round about him realistically, he can hardly avoid seeing the facts with which these Christian terms deal, even though he may prefer to give them some other interpretation. By penetrating deeply into human life and its conditions, as it lies before us in all its reality, we are helped to a deeper understanding of the truth of the divine word. A single example may make this clear. When we read the first pages of the Bible against the background of what our generation has experienced of the godlessness and disintegration of human life, we begin to read them with entirely new eyes. It is the story of man's journey out and away from God. It is not merely a matter of a supposed primeval state, and an event of long ago. It is our own story, the history of our own race. The self-centredness of human life is certainly no myth. The self-seeking individual is no fable. Adam—that is mankind, that is humanity. We are here dealing with something of which we are compelled to say to ourselves: 'You are the subject under consideration.'

It is the same with the content of the Gospel. The word about Christ is not just a lovely story, but hard and unavoidable fact. 'That which we have heard, that which we have seen with our own eyes, that which we have looked at and put our own hands on, that we preach: of the Word of Life we speak. For the Life was revealed and we have seen it; and we witness thereof and preach to you that Life which is eternal, which was with the Father and was revealed to us' (I John 1.1f.). 'It was not some cleverly invented fables which we followed, when we proclaimed to you the power and advent of our Lord Jesus Christ, but we had ourselves seen his glory' (II Pet. 1.16). That which happened to Christ 'did not take place in some secluded corner' (Acts 26.26), but right in the midst of our world, right in the midst of the clear daylight of reality. Just as human selfishness and sin are plain reality, so also is God's love plain reality, revealed in this world through Jesus Christ. That which is told of Christ is not merely a story of something which happened nearly two thousand years ago. It is a present reality. Christ—that is God's way to us, and thereby lies our way back to God. Christ, the second Adam—that is mankind, that is humanity, but, *now* the redeemed humanity, reconciled with God. Here also, without reservation, the saying applies, 'You are the subject under consideration.'

That message which we are to present is a message about Christ. It is the message that, since we belong to Him, we need no longer be slaves of the hostile powers which hold men under their tyranny. God's love and mercy have provided for us through Christ deliverance and freedom. He is our Lord, under whom we may enjoy 'the glorious freedom of the children of God.' Christ has not just come and preached to us about God's love. He has in His sacrifice given us God's love. He has not just proclaimed freedom, but actually made us free. That freedom is now offered to us through the Gospel. Whenever the Gospel is preached, it comes to pass ever anew that Christ is present with His deliverance. The Gospel about Christ is the power of God, which frees us slaves and reconciles us with God.

In recent times much has been said, and that rightly so, about the eschatological character of the Gospel. For that matter, it can be said that the Gospel in its entirety is an eschatological message. Manifestly, of course, in this context the word 'eschatological' is not taken in its narrower meaning, as though it referred merely to 'the doctrine of the last things' of conventional dogmatic theology. It is taken rather in its more extensive meaning, in which the New Testament often uses the word, as when it is said, '*Now* are the last times' (I John 2.18). The Gospel is everywhere shot through with a mighty emphasis upon *now*. We who live in the time of the New Testament are given to experience something which previous generations were not given to experience: 'Blessed are the eyes which see what you see. For I say to you, many prophets and kings wished to see what you see, but were not permitted to see it, and to hear what you hear, but were not permitted to hear it' (Luke 10.23f.). For a long time God had foreshown that in the last time, 'in the fullness of time,' He Himself would intervene for the salvation of His people. For that generations had waited; in hope had they reached out toward that salvation. But from that hour in which Jesus Christ came it can be said, *now* it has become a reality, *now* it is the last time, *now* a new age has burst in upon us, the æon of Righteousness and Life. 'While God previously spoke to the fathers through the prophets, he has *now* in the last time spoken to us through his Son' (Heb. 1.1f.). Deliverance through Christ was foreseen by God before the world's beginning, 'but only *now* in the last times has he been revealed' (I Pet. 1.20). That secret, 'which previously had been unannounced for all eternity, has *now* been revealed' (Rom. 16.25f.). Through Christ God has established a new covenant (I Cor. 11.25; II Cor. 3.6), has made us the 'children of the promise' (Gal. 4.28), and has allowed us to 'taste the powers of the coming æon' (Heb. 6.5).

All too long has this eschatological emphasis on *now* which at once recognizes that great new thing which has come in with Christ, and also holds its perspective open toward that which still remains and will be revealed only in glory—all too long has this eschatological emphasis on *now* been weak in the preaching of our Church. In the New Testament it is by no means weak, and the New Testament message is that which we should send abroad to the people of our time. Here recent theological research has done the Church an invaluable service by drawing attention to the eschatological character of the Gospel's message. Because of this it is much easier for us now to see what actually is expected of the Church's preaching: that the message of that deed which God wrought through Christ shall go forth to all peoples and all men, and carry out its liberating work.

But if our only task, then, is that of merely proclaiming this message, the questions arise, 'Is this not a task which can rather quickly be completed? Is there any real need of its being preached year in and year out? It is, after all, a rather simple and brief message which would be worn out after being preached a short while.' Yes, it could seem that way. But, in fact, the situation is exactly the opposite, because the proclamation of this message is an act through which something happens. It is an act which continues and is never complete as long as this age or æon endures. The superficial observer may imagine that from the standpoint of its actual content the message can quickly be emptied out. But in reality it can never be adequately proclaimed and expounded. When God through Christ snatches us out from the dominion of Sin and Death and sets us down in the new context of Righteousness and Life, that means a totally new creation of the whole of life. 'If any man is in Christ he is a new creation.' Everything receives a new meaning. Consequences of that newness reach into every phase of our existence. Here preaching has its enormous field upon which it must deploy its forces. It may neglect no aspect of the new life's reality. The idea is certainly not that preaching should consist merely in the continuous repetition of the word concerning our deliverance from the dominion of the powers of destruction. To be sure, that must remain the central and the ever recurring motif of all Christian preaching. But it is also required that we make clear what that deliverance and liberation concretely mean. Consequently, the minister-messenger can with full right, and in its deepest meaning, say of himself that nothing human is or may be alien to him. He must in his preaching be familiar with both the heights and the depths of human life, familiar with the tragedy of human life as it finds itself in bondage to the powers of destruction. Likewise, he must be familiar with that glorious freedom of the children of God which is to be possessed in Christ Jesus our Lord.

From another standpoint also it becomes clear how idle is the notion that this message could quickly enough be despatched and finished off. This notion is based on a false intellectualistic conception of the function of the word, as though it were merely a matter of some abstract information. Instead, the Gospel is God's power which goes out over the world in order to carry out its saving work.

That, then, is the glad message which we have been commissioned to preach on God's behalf. Ought we not then to rejoice, and deem it a joy to have a part in the spreading of that Gospel over the earth? To preach the Gospel is certainly no heavy and gloomy task, but rather one filled with joy. How light ought not our feet to be as we come with such a message. Or—with reference to the passage cited earlier from Isa. 52.7—how lively ought not our footsteps to be as we are sent to preach peace, and bring good news, and say, 'Thy God is now king.' The powers of destruction are overthrown. They no longer have us in their power. We are free. We no longer stand under these alien lords and tyrants. Now it is another who is 'our Lord,' Jesus Christ. Even though, as long as this old age lasts, we have a constant fight with the powers of destruction, the conflict is not therefore hopeless. The victory is already won through Christ, and therefore we may even now in an initial way join our voices in that song of praise which we hear pealing out from the land of fulfilment, 'Now have the salvation and the power and the kingdom become our God's, and the authority his Anointed's' (Rev. 12.10). That is the right eschatological now, at once present and coming.

Now is the last time. Salvation has come. The power which is stronger than the powers of destruction has been revealed. God's kingdom is at hand. The authority belongs to God's Anointed. That we already possess here, in the midst of this world of strife. But at the same time it points beyond to the world of fulfilment where Christ —'after he had deprived all the princes and all the potentates and the powers of their might,' and when 'the last of his enemies, death, also was dispossessed of his might'—then turns over the kingdom to God, so that God becomes all in all (I Cor. 15.24–8).

Thus the work of Christ and the message concerning Him comprehends our entire existence, and makes its way from eternity through time and back to eternity. That salvation which was grounded in God's eternal decree, and which from eternity remained an unuttered secret, became through Christ a revealed actuality among us, and that deliverance which He granted us is an eternal deliverance.

IV

THE GOSPEL IN
PREACHING

WE HAVE been considering the nature of the Gospel message. It is upon this message about Christ that the Christian faith depends. For 'how can they believe on him of whom they have not heard? And how can they hear if no one has preached? And how can preachers come if they have not been sent? So faith comes by preaching, but preaching in the power of the word of Christ' (Rom. 10.14, 15, 17). In order that men may come to faith in Christ, and through faith's vital union with Him be delivered from the bondage of the old æon and introduced into the new æon, the age of righteousness and life, for that purpose God has sent out messengers who are to preach—that is, to bear the news of Christ. It is not by mere chance that our divine service in essence takes the form of preaching. Without the preaching of the word there is no divine worship.

When the Augsburg Confession, in its fifth article seeks to define the 'Church's ministry,' and indicate its nature and function, its uses a double expression. The function of the ministry is (1) to preach the Gospel, (2) to administer the sacraments. These two stipulations are equally essential if one is to discuss aright the Church's ministry. First, then, let us examine the nature of preaching, and how the Gospel message is to come forth in it.

If it is not mere chance that that which is utterly essential in the divine service is the proclamation of the word, preaching, so likewise it is no mere accident that preaching takes the form of preaching upon a text, a Biblical text. This also has its reason in the Gospel's character of a message. If the meaning of divine service were only that of inducing in the congregation some generalized religious sentiment, no text would be needed. But just because the divine service has for its meaning the bringing of a message from God, preaching has for its basis a specific passage of Scripture. The text then represents the divine word which is to be brought to the congregation through preaching. The preacher is not to bring forth his own word, and his own ideas, but he comes as a messenger for another. He has a message which is to be delivered with just exactly that content which the sender has stipulated. The word which he is to proclaim is not of the sort which is supplied with such preambles as: this is what I say, this is what I think, or, this is what this or that human authority thinks. Rather, concerning this word it must be said: 'thus saith the Lord.' When preaching is firmly based upon a Biblical text it means just this, that it is a divine message which is to be proclaimed. The sole function of preaching is to make the message and its nature clear, understandable, relevant and living.

As has already been said, preaching, even though it is based upon a text, can never stop with a bare 'textual exposition.' To be sure, a correct interpretation of the content of the text is an utterly essential preparation. Consequently, he who is to preach the word must ever regard it as one of his most important tasks so to steep himself in the Bible that it becomes truly familiar to him. But the more that becomes true the less possible will it be for him to handle a given passage as an isolated 'text,' as though it were his function purely and simply 'to expound.' Rather the text becomes part of a living message which God desires to have proclaimed to His people. Yet the preaching situation is not that we have before us an ancient text, separated from us by several thousand years, and that our task is now that of interpreting and explaining it for some sort of antiquarian interest. Preaching has an entirely different purpose to serve. In preaching the hearer is to perceive God's living voice. He is to hear the word from God as personally directed to him. In that way he is transformed from being a mere auditor to becoming a man addressed by God, from being a mere passive observer to becoming a recipient of the divine message.

The texts upon which preaching is based are then to be so handled that they retain their true evangelical character —the character of a message. An invaluable aid to this end is the arrangement of these texts in the great context of the Church year. Thereby the ever present danger of using random texts is forestalled. In fact the Church year with its series of Biblical selections gives a most splendid witness to the character of the Gospel as a message. He who preaches upon texts of his own choosing can, without difficulty, preach Sunday after Sunday upon his own hobbies. He who preaches on the selections to be found in the series of the Church year, and *truly* preaches on them, he preaches the Gospel about Christ.

For the most part, the value of the Church year is conceded. The only question is: have the deepest foundations of this value been seen? Oftentimes men have been content with a greater or lesser amount of romantic observations about how the Church has celebrated its great days all through the ages. But that is not the point. Again, objections to the traditional Church year have not been lacking entirely. Occasional theologians of a rationalizing type have registered displeasure and have come forward to attack. 'Why don't you begin the Church year by preaching about the creation of the world, and then go through the Christian system of doctrine point by point, so that you cover the whole of it in the course of the year? That way you would reach a sort of conclusion, at the end of the year, in the doctrine of the last things, i.e. eschatology.'

It will not require many words to confute such a rationalistic conception. At the same time, neither can the romantic conception be called satisfactory. The greatest value of the Church year consists in this, that in a surpassing way it gives expression to the divine word's character as a message, and that it so clearly asserts the '*now*-character' of the Gospel which we noted earlier. All that the Gospel has to tell is welded into one in this now present reality. The collects give no less expression to this essential character of the Gospel. The collect for Christmas Day reads, 'O Lord God, who made *that holy night* to be lighted by the glory of the true light'; the collect for Epiphany reads, 'O Lord God, who on *this day* led the heathen by the stars unto thine only-begotten Son, Jesus Christ'; the collect for Candlemas Sunday reads, 'O almighty, eternal God, whose only-begotten Son was on *this day* presented before thee in the temple'; the collect for Easter Day speaks of 'Jesus Christ, our Lord, who on *this day* won the victory over death and opened to us the way to eternal life.'

In the Gospel it is never a question merely of things past, but always of such things as are at the same time present realities in our midst. The Gospel of Christmas, Easter, and Pentecost comes with a message about something which once happened, and yet something which makes its effects felt right in our present-day life. The Incarnation, Christ's Death and Resurrection, His victory over death and the way opened unto life, all these are active realities in the Church of Christ, which is His 'body.' The body has a part in all that befalls Him who is the Head of the Church.

But just how is this at one and the same time past and present to be understood? A certain type of theology, deeply influenced by Kierkegaard, is accustomed to using in this context the expression 'contemporaneity' with Christ. Beyond doubt there is some propriety in this expression even though it is essentially improper. The difficulty with the term is simply this, that when one talks about our contemporaneity with Christ, it is easy to get the impression that time itself has somehow been eliminated, and that it no longer plays any real role. But, that would rob the problem under discussion of its reality. This world in which we live is the world of time, and in this world time neither can nor may be eliminated.

That which happened to Christ took place at a definite point in human history, at that point of time which is called the 'completion of time.' We modern men live in another likewise definitely fixed time, which is separated from the time in which Christ lived His earthly life by more than 1,900 years. It is not our business either to explain away or to blur that intervening span of time. On the contrary, this time separation is constitutive for our life, even for our Christian life. God is the God of time and of history, who actually has a history with His people, a history characterized by a before and an after, by an earlier and a later. That means that we must take time with all seriousness and on no account seek to eliminate it. Attempts to get rid of time spring from platonizing modes of thought, and have no rightful place in the Christian faith.

The past and the present are brought together through preaching, and that because preaching takes the form of a message. Preaching tells of something which once happened but which at the same time means the complete transformation of the conditions of our present life. We ourselves and our destiny were involved in that which was done through Christ. So we are now able in the Church year to experience ever anew that which took place for us and to us.

'In the sacred year of the Church the Christian congregation experiences through a cycle God's redemptive act in Christ. Various ages have contributed to the forming of this Christian year. It is a noble work of art upon which many generations have laboured.' These are the words with which the Church of Sweden's service book begins.

But if it be true, as it is here said, that different ages have contributed to the formation of this work of art, it may well be asked if this Church year actually does have any such unified purpose and any such clear character of a message as has just been asserted. For that matter, many would perhaps question its significance as a work of art. Is not, after all, the Church year a rather simple and artless structure which, in the main, follows the Gospel narrative? Just as the Gospels begin with the story of John the Baptist who prepared the way, so the Church year begins with the time of Advent, the time of preparation. Then follow the stories of Jesus' birth, circumcision, His appearance in the temple at the age of twelve, etc.—all either in chronological order or else in the order used by the evangelists—up to the death of Jesus, His Resurrection and Ascension, and the founding of the Church on the first day of Pentecost. What is there of artistry in that simple historical presentation?

The best answer to that is that there is no antithesis whatever between a work of art and simple historical reality. It is just this intimate connection with those mighty historical realities which meet us in the Gospels, that makes the Church year the work of art that it is. Just because it has no purpose other than that of making it possible for the congregation to experience, as a present reality, in the course of the year, that history upon which its life is based, can the Church year appear in that simple and sublime form which it assumes. Even if the Church year does follow in detail the sequences of the Gospel narrative, that in no way detracts from its value as a pattern for the Christian message.

Nevertheless, it must be added that this talk about following in detail is in the highest degree misleading. The Church year is based upon an original idea which is decisive for its entire architectonic structure. This central theological idea, this conception of the import of the Christian Gospel, meets us at the very beginning, in the Advent message. It is not true that the Advent season is only a time of preparation for the festival of Christmas, and, so to speak, merely for the purpose of recounting the prelude to the Gospel. The Sundays in Advent do not deal just with preparation and with John the Baptist; they have a far more decisive position for the entire Church year. Note the first Sunday in Advent. If the purpose of the Church year were merely that of following the historical sequence, why should the Gospel lesson on this the first day of the Church year be a passage which in its historical context really belongs to Palm Sunday? In fact, this lesson is the Synoptic parallel to Palm Sunday's lesson from the Gospel according to John. Why has this passage been torn out of its historical context and placed at the beginning of the Church year? The answer lies in the dominant idea which pervades the Church year from beginning to end. It is the Gospel's eschatological message which is thus set in the foreground.

One marvels as he reflects upon the fact that this Advent Gospel has stood there at the entrance to the Church year all down the ages—even during that period when those within the Church had forgotten, for the most part, the eschatological import of the Gospel. Even in that period the congregation, on the Church year's first day, united in acclaiming, 'Hosannah to the Son of

David! Blessed is he who comes in the name of the Lord. Hosannah in the highest!' Right against the dominant spirit of the times the congregation was compelled to listen to the eschatological message. For in that acclamation God's people are hailing their Messiah. He is hailed as the One who now stands among us. Now is the last time. The old has passed away; behold, something new has come. It is the 'now-character' of the eschatological message which is so strongly asserted in the Gospel lesson for the first Sunday in Advent. Exactly the same thing meets us in the Epistle lesson which is taken from Rom. 13: 'The night is far spent,' the old æon is coming to a close. 'The day is at hand,' the new æon in an initial stage has already broken in upon us through the coming of Christ. Therefore it is said, 'Now, is the time to awake from sleep.' For us, who through Christ belong to the new day, it is time to 'lay aside the deeds of darkness and clothe ourselves in the armour of light.' It is time to forsake the ways of the old æon and to be recreated in conformity with the new æon and thereby 'put on the Lord Jesus Christ.'

While the first Sunday in Advent thus lays hold on the one side of this eschatological message—namely, on its now-character—the second Sunday in Advent takes up the eschatological future-perspective and speaks of Christ's return in glory. He who in the promise is called 'he who should come' is for the Christian congregation at one and the same time 'he who has come' and 'he who shall come.' This duality in the eschatological message is apparent even in the first two Sundays of the Church year. Here a mighty blow is sprung from Christ's first coming, in lowliness and humiliation, to His return, 'with great power and glory,' from the initial inbreaking of the new æon to its eternal completion.

The Gospel lesson for the third Sunday in Advent carries, in our service book, the title 'Jesus' witness concerning John.' In actuality, however, the import of the passage is much more of a witness to Jesus as the promised Messiah. When John sends the question to Jesus: 'Are you the one who should come, or shall we wait for some other one?' we recognize in the words 'the one who should come' a reference to Him who according to God's promise was to come with the fulfilment of all that which had been promised to the fathers. We recognize here a reference to the Messiah. And when Jesus answers, 'Go back and tell John what you saw and heard,' that implies a clear vindication of His messianic office. For what had they seen and heard? 'The blind receive their sight, the lame walk, the lepers are cleansed, the deaf hear, the dead rise up, and "to the poor is proclaimed the message of gladness" '—in other words, exactly those signs which were to appear at the time of the inbreaking of the messianic æon and which were to give to it their impress. For the messianic time is the æon of resurrection and life. And to the extent that this passage deals with a witness concerning John, it also deals with a witness to the Messiah, since John's task is wholly summed up in 'preparing the way' *for the Messiah*. John points away from himself. He is merely the voice of one who cries. He points to that One who is greater than he (the fourth Sunday in Advent).

Then comes Christmas with its message of joy to those

who live in the land of the shadow of death, that the light of God's splendour has arisen over the earth. It comes with the message of Him who hurls the powers of destruction from their throne and gives us freedom, who breaks asunder the yoke of ancient bondages, the scourge of guilt, the rod of torment, and in their stead sets up His kingdom which is righteousness and peace. Christmas comes with its message, 'To-day a Saviour has been born to you in the city of David, and he is the Messiah, the Lord.' Now it can in truth be said that God has visited His people, and where God is, there is His 'glory.' 'The glory of the Lord shone round about them.' In Christ God erected His tabernacle among men. 'Behold, now God's tabernacle stands among men, and he shall dwell among them, and they shall be his people; yes, God himself shall be with them.' These words from Rev. 21.3 concerning the new heaven and the new earth have had their application in an initial way ever since the Incarnation of Christ. 'He dwelt among us, and we saw his glory.'

In Christ the two convenants are met, the old covenant and the new. He Himself was put under the law, but that was done in order that He might redeem us and give us the right of sonship (the Sunday after Christmas). In Jesus' name the two covenants are met, the old and the new, with circumcision as the sign of the old covenant, and baptism in the name of Jesus as the sign of the new covenant (New Year's Day, the Sunday after New Year's Day).

'The glory of the Lord,' revealed through Christ, is the theme for Epiphany. 'Behold, darkness covers the earth and clouds the people, but the Lord is arising over you, and his glory is revealed over you. And people shall walk in your light, and kings in the splendour which shines above you' (Epiphany). The glory of the Lord filled the temple when Isaiah received his call to be a prophet, but even greater was the glory which filled the temple when He, who was greater than the temple and who in His time was to break down the temple, at the age of twelve stayed behind in the temple, His Father's house (first Sunday after Epiphany). What point the Gospel lesson for the second Sunday after Epiphany—namely, the story of the marriage at Cana, has in this context has been questioned. The reply is, that the point here also has to do with a revelation of the 'Lord's glory.' We read, 'This was the first sign which Jesus did. He did it in Cana in Galilee and thus revealed his glory, and his disciples believed on him.' The miracle at Cana was not a spectacle, but a 'sign,' one of the distinguishing signs of the messianic æon. This same theme of the power and glory of the Lord finds expression in the lessons for the Sundays which immediately follow.

From Epiphany the way leads to Lent. The congregation is to follow the Saviour on His way to the Cross, the way of God's love. Now all shall be fulfilled. The ransom shall be paid, the eternally valid sacrifice shall be offered, the conflict with the powers of destruction shall be fought to the finish. On Good Friday, the new covenant's great day of atonement, all this can be summed up in the words, 'It is finished.'

But, because Christ thus humbled Himself and was obedient unto death, yes, to death upon the Cross, on that account God has also elevated Him up above all things. Christ's act of sacrifice became His victorious act.

At Easter the new message greets us in its most compact form, 'The Lord is risen.' And in our hearts we reply with the congregation of the early Church, 'The Lord is risen indeed!' He who was crucified in weakness now lives by the power of God. He who during His life here on earth was God's Son, though in lowliness and humiliation, Him has God 'designated God's Son in power since the resurrection of the dead' (Rom. 1.4). For the Resurrection of Christ is the beginning of the new æon of the Resurrection. Here the powers of destruction are all thrown down and deprived of their dominion. Consequently, the Epistle lesson for Easter greets us with the triumphant word, 'Death is swallowed up and victory is won. Thou death, where is thy victory? Thou death, where is thy sting? The sting of death is sin, and the power of sin comes from the law. But thanks be to God who gives us the victory through our Lord Jesus Christ!'

We have now reached the high point itself of the Christian message. In our world death reigns with unchecked might. How has death gotten this position of power? It has gotten it through the agency of sin, through sin which is inseparable from all human action and all human life. Sin is that sting with which the tyrant Death subjugates us. Sin is the instrument by means of which death drives us, as a man drives cattle, 'for the children of men fare just as do the cattle. Just as the cattle die, so also do they die' (Eccles. 3.19). The marvellous thing now is, that we, those subjugated and put in bondage by death, can ask, 'Thou death, where is thy victory? Thou death, where is thy sting?' We can do that, since God has given us the victory through our Lord Jesus Christ.

Death is no longer our lord, but Christ is our Lord. God has elevated Him above all things and given Him that name which is above all names—that is, the name Lord, *Kyrios*.

Now the new creation has begun. We are given to live our life 'in Christ.' And accordingly the remainder of the Church year is a great unfolding of what it means to be in Christ and to live in Him.

These brief suggestions may perhaps be enough to show how the Church year is built upon the Christian message and reflects it in all its richness and power. We have every reason to be grateful that our Church has adopted the Church year in its service book. Thereby we are given the finest conceivable assistance towards making our preaching a real proclamation of the Gospel concerning Christ. Thanks to this fact, we are not thrown upon our own resources with topics and lessons of our own choosing. The Gospel message in all its organic coherence, with all its objective weight, and all its subjective challenge, comes forward visibly to meet us in our service book. Here is our rich store, from which we as Christ's servants, and as stewards of God's mysteries, are to bring out things new and old. It is the old Gospel, but as a message it is ever new. If our eyes are but opened to see the fullness of reality and joy in that message, then it will also become a joy to have a part in spreading it.

What greater or more glorious task could be conceived than that of being participants, as God through His Gospel redeems men from the bondage of the powers of destruction, and saves them in that kingdom where Christ is Lord? And that is the task which is set for our preaching.

V

THE GOSPEL IN
THE SACRAMENTS

THE MINISTRY of the Church is to preach the Gospel and administer the sacraments. Preaching and administering the sacraments are the minister's principal tasks. Yet in the deepest sense it is not a matter of two different things. These two are one. When the word is preached, that means that the Gospel is being presented. When the sacrament is distributed, that likewise means that the Gospel message is being presented. How are these, word and sacraments, related to each other? And how does the Gospel appear in a distinct manner in the sacraments?

It is worth remembering that it is the Lutheran Church's basic confession, the Augsburg Confession, which when establishing the import of the Church's ministry places the preaching of the Gospel and the administration of the sacraments side by side as being equally essential. Within later Lutheranism it has often been hard to find any clear and substantial place for the sacraments. That the proclamation of the Gospel, the preaching of the word, is something essential which cannot be lacking in a Christian Church, is of course for all a self-evident truth. But why are sacraments needed? Is not the word enough? Can there ever be, in an Evangelical

Church, a place for anything else alongside of the word? And so one stands there nonplussed when called upon to give a reason for the sacraments, and to state their province and function in the Christian life and in the worship of the Church.

In order to get one's bearings in this situation, very often refuge has been sought in Luther's word about the sacrament as a 'visible word.' Then that saying is interpreted in such a way that the preached word is actually the only essential word. Next, then, it is said that alongside its essential form the word meets us as 'the word in deed,' i.e. the word in action. Just why it should be necessary and desirable that, alongside of its usual form, the word should appear also in the form of deed, is usually explained by a reference to the great illustrative power of action. If a thing is merely told to me, it is all too easy for it to remain on the abstract and invisible plane. It is altogether different when, at the same time that it is being told to me, it is also brought to my attention in deed. Action affects and operates in a distinct way. It makes that which is told tangible and concrete in a manner which the mere word never could do. Nevertheless, this line of argument never gets one beyond a psychological reason for the appearance of the word in the form of action. Actually, all that has been explained are some gestures which accompany and illustrate the word. The proper significance of the sacrament has by no means been explained.

At times this inability to find any real place for the sacrament has been made into an outright virtue, and reasons of principle are given for it. The Roman

Catholic Church, it is said, is a sacramentarian Church, whereas our Evangelical Church is a Church of the word. No interpretation could be more false. The difference between Evangelical Christendom and Roman Catholicism is not that Catholicism has its centre in the sacrament, and that the Evangelical Church has not. On the contrary, the sacrament is central for both. The difference is this: they differ on the meaning of the sacrament, just as they differ on the meaning of the Gospel as a whole. Luther makes the charge against Roman Catholicism that it does not allow the Gospel to be what it is, but rather alters it to a law and a 'righteousness of works.' Rome changes the Gospel from an act of God and a gift to an act of man's own and his accomplishment. In just the same way, his objection to the Roman doctrine of the sacrament is not that it makes too much of the sacrament, but rather that it does not take seriously enough just what the sacrament is as a sacrament. When Luther sets himself against the Catholic doctrine of the Lord's Supper as a sacrifice, 'the sacrifice of the mass,' he does it simply in order to protect the nature of the Lord's Supper as a sacrament. The Lord's Supper is the testament of Christ, 'this cup is the new testament in my blood.' But a testament, or will, is a gift. Of this gift, says Luther, the papacy has made a sacrificial offering. But these two, a gift which is received and a sacrificial offering which is given, are mutually exclusive. The sacrifice goes from us to God, the testament from God to us. In the Lord's Supper it is God who in Christ stoops down to us. In the sacrifice of the mass we seek to climb up to God in all His majesty and make ourselves acceptable to Him.

Enough, then, has been said to show what folly it is to set the Evangelical Church over against the Roman Church as being the Church of the word over against the Church of the sacrament. To be sure, the Evangelical Church is the Church of the word in the most serious sense of the word. It is the Church which is built solely and only upon the divine word. But, it is also, in the strictest sense of the word, the Church of the sacrament. Luther's opposition is directed against the Roman Church with particular force just because the sacrament, the Lord's Supper, is perverted in its worship. The custom is to differentiate between the sacramental and the sacrificial. The sacramental is what God does, the sacrificial that which we do. Luther's principal objection against the Roman service is that it changes the sacrament into an act of ours. It changes God's sacrament into an offering which we make, a sacrifice which we offer. From a gift of God it makes a service which we perform. But this is only another way of saying that the Evangelical Church, in opposition to the Roman Church, lays claim to being the Church of the sacrament, in the true meaning of the sacrament.

This raises anew, and with increased force, the problem of the function and significance of the sacrament. Why is it necessary in the Evangelical Church that the proclamation of the word and the administration of the sacraments should go hand in hand? Why can the one never dispense with the other? By way of introduction, this question may be answered briefly by pointing to the Gospel's character as a message. Since it is a message which we are commissioned to present, we are to carry out our mission in

67

this double form. In the message the word and the deed form a unity. It is not that we have, on the one hand, to do with a message, a proclaimed word, and that then afterwards this proclamation is brought forth in another form, i.e. the form of deed. It is not that the deed is added in order to make the message more penetrating and convincing. On the contrary, the message itself is a deed. In the previous chapter on 'The Gospel Concerning Christ,' the matter could all be summed up, we found, in these words: 'Each time this message is proclaimed, it means that God begins and completes His deed in us. When the Gospel comes upon the scene, God then and there frees man from the dominion of the powers of destruction, and makes him a member of that new humanity whose Lord and Head is Christ.'

If one but keeps this in mind, then there will no longer be any problem as to why the Gospel appears at once as word and deed, at once in word and sacrament. It is its essential nature which comes to expression in this way. In the message concerning Christ there is never a word that is not likewise a deed, but neither is there ever a deed which is without the word. Just as it would be senseless to ask why we need the word when we have the sacrament, so also it is meaningless to ask why we need the sacrament when we have the word. For only in the unity of both is the full import of the Gospel as a message, which is at the same time a deed, and as a deed, which is at the same time a message, to be found. He who would retain the word, but push the sacrament aside, waters down the word and robs it of its character as a deed. Behind such a pushing aside of the sacrament there usually lies a psychologizing interpretation of the word. But that means that one treats the word as a 'mere word,' and forgets that in reality it is an act of God, God's power unto salvation. Luther says of the water in baptism, 'Without God's word it is only water and no baptism.' In the same manner one can say of the word which is set in contrast to the sacrament, 'Without the sacraments it is only a word, and not the power of God, not God's act for our salvation.' The Gospel is given to us by God in the inseparable unity of word and sacrament. What God has joined together, let not man separate.

That which takes place in the sacraments is that the Lord Christ by them incorporates us into Himself, and makes us living members in the body of Christ, in the Church.

First of all, a word as to how this takes place in baptism. Our problem is, how does the Gospel message concerning Christ come forth in the sacraments and, in this instance, in baptism? The Christian message is briefly expressed in this, that we, who by nature are under the dominion of alien powers, are taken out from under that bondage and brought into His kingdom and may now live our life 'in Christ,' in righteousness and peace. Furthermore, we must remember that this message is not mere word and proclamation, but reality and deed.

What now has baptism to do with that message? We can answer: in baptism it is just that Gospel which encounters us, and that in concrete deed. In baptism God deals with us personally, takes us out from the power of darkness and sets us as members in the kingdom of His Son. Through our natural birth we belong to a race which is subjected to sin and death, and as members of that sinful humanity participate, in every aspect of our being, in all of its conditions. In the same manner we, through baptism, are placed in an entirely new context. We are members in the new humanity whose head is Christ and who in Him participate in God's righteousness and in the life of the new æon, the eternal life. It is for this reason that baptism is called 'the bath of regeneration,' because through it we are born into this new existence which God gave us through Christ. By the natural birth we have been born to a life which, in the final analysis, bears the mark of death. Through baptism, the bath of regeneration, we have been born to life, to the life 'in Christ.'

Baptism is the act of initiation into the Christian life. Through it we are implanted into a fellowship of life with Christ. We are members in the body of Christ, as the Apostle Paul says, 'In *one* Spirit are we all baptized into *one* body' (I Cor. 12.13). In baptism the real incorporation into Christ takes place, that is to say, into His *Death* and *Resurrection*. 'We all who have been baptized into Christ, have been baptized into his death' (Rom. 6.3). But we have also been baptized into participation in His Resurrection. In this context the Apostle speaks of our being 'grown together' with Christ in baptism. 'If we have grown together with him through a similar death, so shall we also be made to grow together with him through a similar resurrection' (Rom. 6.5). It is like when an ingrafted branch grows together with the tree. Through baptism we are ingrafted into Christ and grown together with Him. Just as our life here on earth has been put into a vast context, which in the final analysis dominates us, so it is also with the new context into which we have been set with Christ. 'Now it is no longer I who live, but Christ lives in me' (Gal. 2.20). For when we are members in Christ's body, then that which has happened to Him who is the Head and the First-born has happened also to us. Christ's Death is our death. Christ's Resurrection is our resurrection.

Note here the precise correspondence which exists between Jesus' baptism and our baptism. For Jesus baptism was the act of initiation to His messianic work, and likewise that which comprised His messianic work from beginning to end. Baptism showed Him the way which He must go, that it was the way of suffering, death and resurrection. For the heavenly voice which accompanied His baptism used the initial words of the first of the songs of the 'suffering servant of the Lord' (Isa. 41.2). By baptism, then, Jesus was inducted as the suffering servant of the Lord. His messianic task received beforehand its interpretation. He was solemnly inducted as the Messiah who should suffer. His baptism was a baptism unto death. In conformity with this Jesus speaks again and again of His suffering and His death as a baptism which He had to undergo (Luke 12.50; Mark 10.38). Christ's death upon the Cross was that baptism which He underwent once for all, when He as the Messiah, the suffering servant of the Lord, took our place.

In the same way our baptism is the act of initiation through which we are brought into the messianic people. And yet at the same time it embraces our entire Christian life from beginning to end. Baptism is a baptism unto death, but also unto resurrection. Only by continually dying with Christ and rising with Him can the baptized person remain a living member in Christ, a living branch in the true vine (John 15.1ff.). Christ had died from sin once for all (Rom. 6.10). He who belongs to His body, therefore, has to die away from the 'body of sin' (Rom. 6.6) to which we belong through Adam, i.e. through our belonging to the old æon. Thus, for the Christian it becomes a continual dying with reference to the old man, which has been crucified and shall be crucified (Rom. 6.6), and a constant resurrection with Christ unto the life of righteousness.

No one has seen and described better than Luther how this significance of baptism embraces the whole Christian life. In answer to a question about the meaning of baptism, he answers: 'It means that the old man in us shall, through daily repentance and reformation, be stifled and put to death with all sins and evil lusts, and that a new man shall daily come forth and arise, who shall live in righteousness and holiness before God eternally.' From the time of baptism until death the baptized person is to live his life 'in Christ,' grown together with Him. Consequently baptism carries with it the promise of sharing in the eternal glory of Christ when this 'body of sin and death' has finally been destroyed.

As ministers we are not merely to preach the word, but also to baptize. We are commissioned by Christ to receive men into His fellowship, into participation in His Death and Resurrection, through baptism. Should we otherwise forget this, we have here an unequivocal reminder of the fact that it was in order to carry out a *deed* that Christ has come—namely, to wrest us from the dominion of death and give us His new life, the eternal life. It is for the carrying out of that deed that He desires to use us as instruments.

This message which is likewise a deed appears no less clearly in the Lord's Supper. If baptism is an act which is done but once, which for the first time establishes a connection between our life and Christ, so the Lord's Supper is given to us in order that through it Christ may ever anew build up and nourish those who are members of His body. Just as the Passover was celebrated in commemoration of God's founding act in the old covenant, by the deliverance from Egypt, so the Lord's Supper is instituted for the commemoration of God's founding act in the new covenant, by the atoning death of Christ. 'This cup is the new covenant in my blood. As often as you drink it, do so in remembrance of me. For as often as you eat this bread and drink the cup, you proclaim the Lord's death, until he comes' (I Cor. 11.25f.).

Yet the Lord's Supper is more than a mere commemoration. That which is essential in the Lord's Supper is that Christ Himself is present and builds up His body. When the bread which has been blessed is passed, it is done with the instruction, 'this is the body of Christ' (I Cor. 11.24). Here the Christian comes into immediate contact with his living Lord. Therefore the bread which is broken can be described as 'participation in the body of Christ.' 'The bread, which we break, is it not a participation in Christ's body? Since there is *one* bread, so we, though many, are *one* body, for we all share in that one bread' (I Cor. 10.16f.). All share in Christ who is the Head of the Church, and who in Himself gathers up all and rules over all. In the Lord's Supper life flows forth from Christ and through His body to all its members.

That communion of life with Himself which Christ grants us in the holy sacraments, in baptism and the Lord's Supper, is in its essence a mystery. It is something which we can never entirely penetrate with our thought. Here the Scripture passage applies, 'Your life is hidden with Christ in God' (Col. 3.3). But the mystery which is here spoken of is nothing other than the mystery in the Gospel itself. That mystery is that into this world of death God has introduced Him who is the Prince of life, and that He has called us to be one with Him and to share in His life.

VI

THE GOSPEL IN TEACHING

AS MESSENGERS it is our task to preach the Gospel
and to administer the sacraments. Fundamentally, all
that is essential about the minister's work is said in this.
For where the Gospel is preached purely and the sacraments are administered rightly, there is the Church,
there is the communion of the saints. Where the Gospel
concerning Christ is proclaimed, there is the messianic
people, there the new people of God is present, gathered
about its Lord. And where the sacraments are administered rightly, there Christ is present and builds up His
body. Through baptism new branches are continually
grafted into the vine Christ. Thereby new children are
continually being incorporated into Christ, humanity's
new Head. They become living members in the body of
Christ, living stones in God's temple. In the Lord's
Supper Christ gives Himself to those who are His,
enters into them and becomes life in their life. Through
the preaching of the Gospel and the administration of the
sacraments decisive and fundamental things happen to
us. Our life is taken out of the bondage to sin and death,
and we are incorporated into Christ, who is Himself the

resurrection and the life. Even though in the world we must still continually battle with the powers of destruction, nevertheless, 'in Christ' we may be the 'children of the resurrection.' Actually, in this everything has been said, and nothing more needs to be added.

Consequently, if none the less we now take up for special consideration the question of the Gospel in teaching, that does not mean that to the two things named, the preaching of the word and the administration of the sacraments, a third is to be added for completion's sake. Rather it means simply that we select an especially important phase which is already included in what has previously been discussed. To preach the Gospel aright and to administer the sacraments aright always and necessarily involves an element of teaching. This has been so from the earliest days of Christendom, and it is still ever the same. In fact, it is now even more necessary than ever that the Church truly do all that lies within its power toward increasing Christian knowledge among our people. If the Church in by-gone days could, in large measure, lean upon the home and the school, when it came to communicating Christian knowledge to the rising generation, the assistance to be had from these sources has in recent times steadily dwindled. Even though it is confessed with gratitude that both the home and the school do always mean very much indeed for the Christian nurture of our people, nevertheless the greatest share of the responsibility, more and more, comes to rest upon the Church's own teaching activity. That means that the minister-messenger must also be a minister-teacher.

For this its task of teaching our Church has an invaluable, classic aid in Luther's *Small Catechism*. There is something unusual about this book. Though it appeared more than four hundred years ago, it has preserved its relevance and freshness through the centuries. Time and again it has been supposed that this book could be ruled out and supplanted by something better and more up-to-date. But all these attempts have failed. Luther's *Small Catechism* has survived them all, and the theological research of the most recent decades has contributed toward bringing it again into the foreground. Upon what does this unique vitality depend? The explanation has often been found in Luther's artistic gifts. Beyond doubt there is some truth in that explanation. Whereas most expositions of the Christian faith appear in a dry and abstract doctrinal form, Luther's meets us in a concrete and clear form such as only a born artist can produce. Nevertheless, that is not the whole explanation.

The most basic reason why Luther's *Small Catechism* contains such a perfect training in Christianity lies rather in that he, as no one else did, understood the Gospel simply as a message to us. Moreover, again as no one else could, he was able to give expression to the content of that message in a simple, deft, and easily understood style.

Look for a moment at his explanation of the second article of the Apostles' Creed: 'I believe that Jesus Christ is my Lord, who redeemed me from all the powers of destruction which hold us in bondage. Me, a lost man, who stands under the dominion of death and the devil, has he redeemed, purchased and won. And this he has done through his sacrifice of love, with his innocent suffering and death. Now I am therefore no longer under the violence of the alien powers, but I am his own, who shall live and remain under him in his kingdom and serve him in everlasting righteousness—and all that in the power of his resurrection: as he is risen from the dead, lives and reigns eternally.' Where is there any more simple and appealing exposition of the Christian message?

In the five main sections of the catechism we have a summary of the content of the Christian faith which both plumbs its depths and yet preserves its simplicity. If we ministers have ourselves but found the key to understanding it, then it is not hard to make its contents come alive in teaching for pupils of various ages. It becomes an instruction which is easily grasped by beginners, but at the same time invites the more advanced to ever new depths. It is a 'child's doctrine,' which always has something new to give to even the ripest Christian.

Law and *Gospel* are Christianity's first two chapters. In the Law God's holy will is proclaimed as the law for our life. God, our God, has laid upon us His demand, which we cannot arbitrarily push aside. In the Gospel that which God has given to us is proclaimed. It tells of how 'all things come from God.' He is our creator, from whom we have all that we possess. He is the one who has provided salvation for us in Christ, and who through His Holy Spirit sanctifies us as well as the whole of Christendom on earth. Hence it is clear that God is the one who demands all and gives all. 'Everything comes from God,' and all shall be held for His service. But while Law and Gospel are the most fundamental and basic elements in

Christianity, they are at the same time likewise its deepest problem, one that we can never fully resolve. Luther is right when he says that the highest art in theology consists in rightly distinguishing between Law and Gospel, and that he who has learned this art may thank God and know that he is a genuine theologian. Here the two first sections of the catechism give the minister-teacher cause and opportunity for constant deepening in this the most central task in the Christian faith.

The same is true of the third section of the catechism, that on prayer. What could be more simple than the Lord's Prayer? And yet it can never in any measure be exhausted. Each one who prays, to whatever stage he may have attained, has something essential to learn from that prayer. To this, then, the two final sections of the catechism add. One takes up the topic of our initial incorporation into Christ through baptism. The other deals with our on-going incorporation into Him in the Lord's Supper. Thus we have here a comprehensive picture of the Christian life, a comprehensive proclamation of the Gospel concerning Christ.

These few words, which cannot in the nature of this situation be more than brief hints, will, I trust, serve to quicken our joy in the task of teaching, a joy for which there is every reason in the task itself. Just as when one thinks of the message, the Gospel, which we are commissioned to proclaim, he is made to exclaim, 'How beautiful are the feet of those who bear the tidings of joy,' so also there is every reason and right to say the same when we think of our teaching function. For in essence it is but the same thing in both instances. Teaching is only a special form for the Gospel concerning Christ. The teacher may often enough get the impression that it is a very elementary task that has been given to him, and that the simple sentences of the catechism would soon become exhausted. If, for example, we think of the Apostles' Creed, it can seem as though their short, gem-like sentences, artlessly joined one to the other, would quickly be learned, and that there would not be so much to add later. In actuality the situation is just the opposite. Every line in the Apostles' Creed encloses such a wealth that one could well-nigh unroll from it the whole Christian message.

It would take too long to show this in detail here. I shall restrict myself to illustrating what has been said by a single point. For that purpose the final words of the Creed will suffice, 'I believe in an eternal life.' Eternal life—that is the last, the final goal, toward which the Christian life looks forward. It is the fulfilment of that of which we during our present life have seen only the beginning, the eternal life in God's fellowship.

Having said this, the question at once arises: how can we properly speak of that which we have never seen and of which we have no direct experience? For that matter, how can we in any sense speak about it? Is it not of such a nature as no eye has seen, and no ear heard, and has not arisen in any man's heart? Would it not be best and most right to refrain from expressing oneself about it, rather than coming along with uncertain presumptions and high-flying fantasies? A glance at how the question of eternal life has been handled in the usual expositions of the Christian faith can, for that matter, make us wary.

The problem of 'the last things' has in recent times often been handled with an unusual lack of sympathy. When it has been taken up for more extensive treatment it has usually been done in such a manner that one must say 'the way is forbidding.'

But our New Testament does not avoid this problem; neither does our Apostles' Creed. Moreover, a Christianity which no longer has its perspective open toward eternal life is no longer a real Christianity. Hope is an essential aspect of the Christian life, and hope reaches out to eternal life. 'Faith, hope, love'—these three belong inseparably together in the Christian life. One cannot speak properly of either faith or love if one neglects to speak of hope. In other words, we are compelled to speak of eternal life, compelled for the sake of the truth of the Christian faith.

One difficulty is, however, to be met—namely, that often when eternal life is spoken of one means by the term something totally different from that which the Christian faith means by it. As a preparation to the exposition of this term's Christian significance it will be useful, therefore, to notice some other interpretations.

At times eternal life is spoken of quite simply as meaning a life which never ends. Eternal life then means nothing more nor less than the forever continuing life, that life which is not subject to the ordinary fluctuations of time, nor subject to the law of age and death. Of such an interpretation of eternal life it must, however, be said that it is based upon a decidedly sentimental manner of thinking. Eternity, in the sense of not ceasing to exist in spite of all changes, we usually attribute to those elements of which our material existence is thought to be compounded, whether we call them atoms, units of energy, or some other name. Through their combinations phenomena appear and disappear, but in the midst of these changes they themselves remain, or are thought to remain, as the indestructible basis. Likewise one could perhaps use the word 'eternal' of the laws according to which all these changes transpire. But when one is dealing with life, the situation is quite different. We know of no life which does not follow the scheme of being born, growing, reaching its prime, ageing, and dying. Apart from these successive stages we simply cannot conceive of life. That would mean then that the word 'eternal' really could not be used of life. But here our whole existence rises up in protest. Just when we are confronted with the transitoriness of life, there is something within us which refuses to accept that, and which instead raises the demand for the eternity of life. It is the self-assertion innate in every life which arises in protest against the destruction of life. Life *will* not go under. Using this unwillingness as a starting-point the attempt has often been made to prove that it is impossible for life to be defeated in death. But each and every one of us is immediately aware of the untenability of such a proof. An eternity or immortality so conceived is nothing other than a reflex of our self-assertive will. It is, therefore, just a matter of typical sentimental thinking, or wishful thinking. It is the will to live, which postulates a reality which corresponds to its demand. It is unwilling that death should be the end, and therefore it demands a continuing life on the other side.

By and large this is the basis upon which the natural man's belief in an eternal life rests. But—and this is a matter which ought to be observed carefully—when Christianity speaks of the eternal life, it has nothing whatever to do with such considerations. Its faith in an eternal life has an utterly different significance and meaning, and rests upon an entirely different basis. Briefly and to the point, we could express the matter thus: Christianity does not believe in the eternity of life, rather it believes in the eternal life. For the view just discussed above there would be no distinction between these two beliefs. When it speaks of the eternal life it means simply the eternity of life. It means that life cannot perish, but that it will continue through all eternity. But Christianity does not believe in such an eternity of life. It reckons realistically with the fact of death. It takes death in all seriousness, and knows that our lot is that death shall destroy our life. And when it likewise believes in eternal life, it does so because it believes that the God, who gives us life and allows it to go under in death, shall call us out again from death and give us eternal life. The two last lines in the Apostles' Creed belong, accordingly, together, and only when held together do they give expression to the view of the Christian faith on this problem: 'I believe in the resurrection of the dead and an eternal life.' The words, 'the resurrection of the dead,' belong, of course, to that portion of the Creed to which, in many ways, it is the hardest for us to reconcile ourselves. The words, 'the eternal life,' have, however, been much easier to accept. Into these the natural craving for the eternity of life could forthwith be read. And, furthermore, the ground had been prepared for this through platonic-neoplatonic modes of thought.

It will, therefore, be useful to pause for a moment at this point, simply because the blending of the Christian and the platonizing outlooks has brought about one of the greatest difficulties to be encountered when trying to achieve clarity about the Christian faith in the eternal life. Platonism also knows how to speak about the eternal. It differentiates between two worlds, the lower and the higher world, the world of sense and the world of ideas. The world of sense is the world of transitoriness, where all things are change, instability, appearance, and vanity. The world of ideas, on the other hand, is unchangeable and at rest in itself. To that higher world of eternity man belongs with reference to the higher portion of his being. Death means only that the lower portion of his being, which belongs to the world of sense, is broken down, and that the higher portion is freed and can return to its abode in the higher world. When someone who belongs in the platonic tradition hears the words, 'I believe in an eternal life,' he supposes that in them he recognizes this same platonic viewpoint with its ascetic drive, its contempt for the world of sense, and its longing for the world of ideas. But when alongside of these words he hears those about 'the resurrection of the dead,' he finds himself certainly a bit disoriented.

What then about this juxtaposition of faith in the resurrection of the dead and faith in an eternal life? At times it has been looked upon as a putting together of a decidedly unmatched pair: faith in the resurrection of

the dead, that is the ancient Christian faith; faith in
eternal life, that is the heritage from the ancient classical
world; so it has seemed. And so these two have been
combined with each other, but in such a way that no real
unity can arise. Nevertheless, this is certainly a misinterpretation. Faith in the resurrection of the dead, and
faith in an eternal life, are both alike genuinely Christian.
They lie in direct line with each other. The problem is
simply that of understanding aright the Christian significance of the term 'eternal life,' and of not confusing it
with that significance which the term can have in another
area, and in a non-Christian context.

What, then, is the meaning of the closing words of the
Creed, 'I believe in an eternal life'? What is the Christian
significance of these words? This is perhaps not as easy to
answer if we hold ourselves rigorously to the words of the
Apostles' Creed. It would be easier if we were helped by
the parallel section in the Nicene Creed. This Creed also
closes with the same two lines about the resurrection of
the dead and eternal life. But the advantage with its
formulation is that it uses in the last line an expression
which is well known to us from the New Testament.
The Nicene Creed closes with these words, 'I look
for the resurrection of the dead and the life of the
coming world.' One may not recognize at once, and
precisely, from these words in their modern translation
that they refer to eternal life. In the Greek original,
however, it is much more plain. There the word used is
'æon,' or 'age.' This is the New Testament's word for
eternity. 'The life of the coming world' means, therefore,
the same as 'the coming age,' 'the life of the coming

æon,' 'the eternal life.' And with this the matter is at once clear. For what the coming æon means in the New Testament we know quite well. Now our problem is set in a large context of which we know something definite. It is now fitted into the very heart of the Christian Gospel.

This age and the coming one—these are the two mighty contrasts in human life, as the Christian Gospel sees it. This age, this æon, is the ordinary human life, as it is lived outside of Christ. In this age we all have a share, inasmuch as we share in the ordinary, natural life. But this age is the æon of sin and death. Thus our life is 'in Adam.' All the children of Adam, all mankind live in the world of sin and death, subject to the alien powers of destruction on account of sin (Rom. 5). But now 'in Christ' we also share in the new age, the æon of life. Of him who believes in Christ it is said, 'he who through faith is righteous shall *live*.' To 'be in Christ,' that is to live actually, it means to have 'passed from death to life.'

How then are these two æons related to one another? It would be natural to suppose that the old æon would be wholly past and antiquated, now that the new æon has made its entrance through Christ. And so indeed have fanatical movements been fond of thinking. In general it is characteristic of all fanatical interpretations of Christianity that they dismiss as dreams the actual situation, and imagine that they have already reached the goal. But in reality this world has not ceased to exist because Christ came. He who believes in Christ indeed has his citizenship in heaven, but he still belongs also to this world, this æon.

Thus ever since the coming of Christ into the world the two æons clash and overlap. Before the coming of Christ the new æon rightly bore the name, 'the coming æon,' for then it was something to which one could still look forward as that which would some day come. But now that Christ has come it greets us as a reality already present. God has come to us and taken up His dwelling among us, in the midst of this world of sin and death. Eternal life is already a present reality among us. At the same time that does not mean that it has ceased entirely to be something coming. Through Christ we already possess eternal life, but still only in an initial way. The new æon has broken in, but not yet in glory.

There is a definite parallelism between the life of Christ here on earth and the life of His congregation. As long as Christ lived here on earth He was certainly God's Son, but still so only in weakness and humiliation. Only through the Resurrection did He become, as the Apostle says (Rom. 1.4), appointed by God as 'the Son of God in power.' So also we, through the Resurrection of Christ, have been appointed to be 'the children of the resurrection.' But we possess this only in hope as long as we live in this world of sin and death. It shall be revealed in power and glory only on the day of resurrection.

It has often been regarded as a contradiction that the New Testament speaks of eternal life now as something present, and again as something coming. Moreover, this has been looked upon as a proof of the fact that here different conceptions are in conflict. Nothing could be more erroneous. Only by holding together these seemingly contradictory assertions can we gain any correct picture of the conception of eternal life as held in the Christian faith. Eternal life has come as a reality to our world through Jesus Christ. He who believes in Him already has eternal life. Nevertheless, he does not possess it in its perfection. It is something which has begun, but has not yet reached its fullness. It is like the rosy dawn, which does not just announce the new day, but is itself a part of it, even though the day has not yet reached its noontide height. Just as one can debate over whether the first gleams of light belong to the night or to the day, so one can also question whether the Christian life belongs to this æon or to the coming æon. It is, in fact, lived in the old æon with all its conditions. And yet it belongs to the new æon. It does not merely announce the inbreaking of the new æon, but is rather already a part of it—namely, its beginning.

This then makes it clear that faith in eternal life is not a loose appendix, but an integral part of the Christian faith. Faith in God and faith in Christ *are* faith in eternal life. 'This is eternal life, that they know thee, the only true God, and him whom thou hast sent, Jesus Christ' (John 17.3). So fast anchored, therefore, is this faith in eternal life, that it is the Christian faith itself.

Consequently, the Christian faith is unwilling to insert anything into the hope of eternal life other than that which already is included in faith in Christ. Eternal life is nothing other than the completion of that life which Christ introduced into the world. When one speaks of eternal life in other terms, he must be ready to give free rein to religious fantasy. The Christian faith, however, speaks with complete sobriety about eternal life. It knows some utterly certain things about that life, since it has come to us through Jesus Christ. But on the other hand it knows very clearly each boundary of its knowledge, and thereby also knows the bounds of its right to speak on this subject. Both of these aspects are brought together in a superlative manner in I John 3.2, 'We are now the children of God, and what we shall be is still not revealed. But this we know, that when he is finally revealed, we shall be like him.' Note how fast anchored the Christian faith in the eternal life is in that which we already possess through Christ. 'We are now the children of God.' How can we assert that with such certainty? Because God has sent His Son into the world, and because we now through faith belong to Him. 'To all those who received him gave he power to be the children of God, to those who believe on his name' (John 1.12). Such is the present, and that is something which we know. But what will eternal life be like? We know nothing about that. 'What we shall be is still not revealed.' In his original and sure fashion, Luther says in one place, 'It is with us Christians as with a babe in its mother's womb. How could it have any conception of the life which it goes to meet?' Indeed, so it is with us Christians. How can we fashion for ourselves a valid conception of what that eternal life is like, which we go to meet? Is then every thought and every idea here equally justified or equally unjustified? Has then the Christian faith nothing more to say to us concerning what eternal life is? Has it no compass to give us? Yes, one thing we do know with full certainty, 'this we know, that when he is finally revealed, we shall be like him.'

Our faith in the eternal life is exactly the same as our faith in Christ. The Gospel concerning the eternal life is exactly the same as the Gospel concerning Christ. Because we belong to Him and live in Him, that which has happened to Him is true also of us. He has died; therefore we are called to die with Him. He has risen; therefore we are called to rise with Him. He lives; we shall also live. But our lives still belong essentially to that which is hidden. 'You have died,' says the Apostle, 'and your life is hidden with Christ in God.' Such is the Christian's situation as long as this æon endures. The eternal life, which he possesses, is a life hidden with Christ in God. But at length that which is hidden shall be revealed. So the Apostle continues: 'But when Christ, he who is our life, is revealed, then shall you also with him be revealed in glory' (Col. 3.3f.).

From faith in Christ, then, the Christian faith in eternal life and the Christian hope of eternal life receive their content and their character. This Christian faith in eternal life is not merely faith in an endlessly continuing life, not purely and simply faith in a continued existence after death. It is not a belief that life as such is stronger than death. Rather it is faith in the God who is stronger than death, and faith in the Lord who arose from the dead. It is, to use the words of Eph. 1.19ff., faith in 'the mighty strength of power by which God has wrought in Christ, in that he raised him from the dead and set him on his right hand in the heavenly world, over all the princes of the spiritual world, and powers, and forces, and lords, yea, over all that can be named, not only in this æon, but also in the coming one. . . . And gave him to the congregation' to be its Head and make it a partaker of all that He possesses.

VII

THE GOSPEL AND
THE CHURCHES

THE CHURCH is the body of Christ. How then
can one speak of several Churches? Just as there is one
Christ, so there can be but one body of Christ. Does it
not follow from this that there can be only *one* Church?
And, furthermore, the Gospel concerning Christ is a
single and unitary Gospel. Must not the Church then,
which is to proclaim that unitary Gospel, itself also be
one?

It is indeed a serious problem with which this question
confronts us. And it becomes doubly serious when we
regard the matter from the perspective of the Gospel.
There is only one name under heaven, given among
men, through which we can be saved, the name Jesus
Christ. It is to proclaim that one name, and to proclaim
that unambiguous Gospel concerning Him, that the
Church of Christ exists. But if we glance out over the
world that which greets our eyes is not the picture of a
single and unitary Church. Instead we find a string of
different Churches or confessions, which—even though
each and every one asserts that it is proclaiming the
Gospel concerning Christ—interpret that Gospel and the

work of Christ in a different manner, and lead men into different ways of salvation. This then raises the question: is not the one Gospel a judgment upon the many Churches?

That the one Church of Christ appears in such a shattered form, so that one must speak of several different Churches, is, from one standpoint, an indication of the power of sin within the Church. We have every reason to ask, with the Apostle Paul, 'Is Christ then divided?' No, the causes for the dissensions and schisms within the Church lie not in Christ, but in His weak disciples and followers; not in the Gospel, but in the frailty of those who are to bear the Gospel. Even though it can be said that the riches of the Gospel are so immeasurably great that no single Church can assert that it has grasped their full and complete meaning, nevertheless that in no way leads necessarily to the splitting up of the Church—were not sin involved. In the dissensions between the various Churches there lies an abundance of false human ambition and sinful, self-assertive wilfulness, which stands in the way of the evangelical message and its work in the world. By no means least, the disunion of the Church is a serious scandal in the eyes of those who stand outside it.

To many the problem of 'the Churches' seems easy enough to solve, provided that one could reckon with a little goodwill from the various sections. If the various Churches or confessions, instead of meeting each other with self-assertion, the will-to-power, and suspicion, could meet in love, and trust, and open brotherliness, those things which divide could easily be gotten rid of. If only each Church were willing to give up something of its own tradition, and be persuaded to listen to the others, and to learn from them, the longed-for unity of the Churches would soon be achieved.

It can, to be sure, happen that way. But the problem has another side also, and there again the consideration of the Gospel has something important to say to us. 'That they all may be one'—it is that for which our Saviour prays on behalf of His Church (John 17.21). But the way to the unity of the Church runs not merely through brotherly love, but also through fidelity to the Gospel which has been entrusted to us by God. The very thought that the unity of the church could be achieved through a compromise between the various Churches, and that thereby they would make reciprocal approaches to one another, indicates that it has been completely forgotten that we are only messengers. The Gospel which we are to bear is not our own, as though we, at our discretion, could have it at our disposal and give up this or that part of it. The Gospel is God's and thereby we are deprived of our right of disposal. God has given us His Gospel, the Gospel concerning Christ. That is the Gospel which we are to bear. When the various 'Churches' or confessions interpret that Gospel in different ways, there is no meaning to the question—if, of course, one understands the situation correctly—how shall we be able to harmonize these different interpretations, in order that we may all come to agreement. Rather, the question must be: what was *His* meaning who sent out the Gospel? Here the one confession assumes the significance to another of the question: has the one truly understood the Gospel in its deepest meaning and in its full import?

The disunity of Christendom is in itself a summons to enter deeper into the truth of the Gospel. Truly the hymn has it:

> Let more and more a scattered host
> United be in thy truth's light,
> That there may be, forever be
> One *shepherd* and one *fold*.

It is in the light of truth that unity shall be achieved. The unity of the Church is not furthered by offering any realized truth, but rather by penetrating deeper into the truth.

Our Evangelical Lutheran Church had its origin in such a deeper penetration into the truth of the Gospel. Within the Church of Christ the Gospel concerning Christ has been preached throughout the years. There has never been a time when the Gospel was entirely lost. But sometimes the Gospel appeared in great clarity, and sometimes mingled with a multitude of things derived from other sources. Consequently, it was hard to understand the right meaning of the Gospel. Luther found the Church in this confused situation. He had no intention of founding a new Church, nor did he do so. What he desired was to give back to the Church the Gospel in its purity. The fact that the Gospel had become for him a living message, a personal word from the living God, this was that which drove him out on to the way of reformation. For if indeed it is a message from God, what can be more urgent than that we should learn to know and to understand that message in its proper and original meaning, and that it be purely and clearly proclaimed to the congregation? If

God actually has dealt with us in Christ, and if He has sent out the Gospel concerning Him through whom atonement and redemption came to pass, what can be more important than that this Gospel, in unadulterated form, should reach men and carry out its redeeming work in them? This is the ground for Luther's constant emphasis upon 'the Scriptures alone,' and 'by faith alone.' When he continually tries anew to get back to the Word, he does so because there he meets the divine Gospel. It is dictated by his concern that God's Gospel shall sound forth clearly and undiminished. Moreover, in regard to the doctrine of 'justification by faith alone,' this is not a mere doctrine. It is just that eschatological Gospel concerning Christ, and of how God through Christ takes us out from the dominion of sin and death, and gives us righteousness and life.

From this it is clear that our Evangelical Lutheran Church bears that name, not as though it were something other than a Church of Christ, or as though, alongside of the universal Christian faith, it was to cherish certain doctrines peculiar to itself. It has no private and independent Gospel beside the Christian Gospel. Rather, it asks only that the Gospel shall be taken with all seriousness, and be presented in its original meaning. Just as there is but one Christian Gospel, so there is also but one Church, the Church of Christ. It is of that Church that we, in the third section of the Creed, confess, 'I believe in one holy, universal church, the communion of saints.' We thank God that He has made us ministers in that one Church of Christ—in order that we may preach the Gospel of our Lord Jesus Christ. We thank Him also that He through

His servant Martin Luther opened the eyes of His Church to see the overwhelming glory of that Gospel.

Simply because our Evangelical Church wishes nothing else than the Gospel, and that pure and clear, it may by being faithful to the basic thought of the Reformation on 'the Scriptures only,' and 'by faith alone,' in the very deepest sense contribute to the union of Christendom. For unity is already given to us in Christ. The unity lies in the evangel, in the Gospel concerning Him.

VIII

THE GOSPEL AND
THE WORLD

ONE LAST question remains, the question of 'the Gospel and the world.'

To whom is it that the Gospel addresses itself? To the people of Christ, to those who believe in Christ? Yes, to these, of course. From this, however, the conclusion has often been drawn that the Gospel should be addressed only to a limited circle. It has been supposed that the Church's message has reference, properly, to only the small flock of the believers, because the world outside, strictly speaking, has nothing to do with the Gospel, just as the Gospel has nothing to do with the world.

This conception must, however, be regarded as basically erroneous. We who have been commissioned to preach the Gospel concerning Christ may never forget that this Gospel addresses itself not merely to a certain group of men, but to the world, to the world in its entirety. 'God so loved *the world*, that he gave his only-begotten Son, that each one who believes in him shall not perish, but have eternal life' (John 3.16). It is the world, all that is called man, that through sin has come under the powers of destruction. So also it is the world which is the subject of Christ's salvation. Note how the purpose of sending

Christ is stated in the verse which follows immediately upon the one just quoted, 'in order that *the world* through him might be saved' (John 3.17). Let us never lose sight of the world-wide, world-encompassing character of our Gospel. Our Saviour is the Saviour of the world. Therefore the Gospel concerning Him belongs to the world. He who is 'our Lord' is also the world's Lord. When bidding His disciples farewell, the risen Lord said, 'All power is given to me in heaven and on earth' (Matt. 28.18). This, His dominion over the world—still hidden, it is true, as long as this æon endures—is the basis for that Gospel which He now sends forth, 'Go ye therefore out.' 'Go out *into the whole world* and preach the gospel *for all that is created*' (Mark 16.15).

Our world lies under the domination of the powers of destruction. But through Jesus Christ the new creation has begun. His Resurrection marks the decisive turning-point, not only in His own life—from humiliation to exaltation—but also in the life of humanity, and, we may add, the turning-point even in the total progress of the world. That which has happened to Him as the first-born shall also happen to those who through faith are incorporated with Him. Yet our New Testament teaches us further, that the destinies of mankind and of the world are inseparably linked together. Just as not only we, but the whole 'creation has been laid under futility,' so also the whole creation with us longs for the final redemption (Rom. 8.19–23). The goal toward which the Christian faith and the Christian hope look forward is not only the new man who is created unto likeness with God in righteousness and holiness, not alone the new man who stands under the righteousness of God. 'According to his promise, we look for new heavens and a new earth wherein righteousness dwells' (II Pet. 3.13).

The thought of Christ as the Saviour of the world who has come, and as the coming Perfecter of the world, should be able to free our Gospel from all narrowness. The Gospel concerning Christ belongs to all. It knows no boundaries. The messengers, accordingly, go out into the whole world in the work of missions. Consequently, we also must break down all the artificial barriers which exist between the Christian and the world. God is not the God only of those who believe in Him. We are all in His hands, whether with our faith or with our un-belief. He who does not believe also stands under God— under God's law—whether he knows it or not. But then the Gospel also, the message of redemption and freedom through Christ, is intended for him. It addresses itself to him and appeals for faith.

It is said of the work of Christ, 'It is finished.' Yet the message concerning Him and His work goes farther out from generation to generation, never finished, never accomplished, as long as this æon endures. We who are commissioned to proclaim the Gospel—our task is that as 'God's fellow-labourers' we should carry the work forward.

There is nothing of which our Evangelical Church is so afraid as any mention of our co-operation with God in the work of salvation. Without reservation, it is asserted that 'everything comes from God.' There is no place here for any human co-operation with God. All 'synergism' is in principle rejected.

When it comes to the work of spreading the Gospel, however, the situation is utterly different. Here God desires to have us with Him as His co-labourers. All is accomplished—but still something is lacking until this Gospel has reached out to all and has been received by the elect. Here He calls us into His service and says, 'Whom shall I send, and who will be our messenger?' What greater mission could be conceived, what more full of responsibility? God has bound His work up with our work. It can depend upon our faithfulness and our zeal whether or not God's work shall prosper.

If that were all that there was to say on this subject, then the messenger's task would be a heavy, an inhumanly heavy task. Who would dare to take upon himself that mission, if in the end it depended upon his own ability and faithfulness? Yet it is not we ourselves who take upon us this task. The Lord says, 'Go forth. Lo, I send you' (Luke 10.3). And when that is done, there is no longer any problem of human ability and human preference. When the Lord sends out, He gives whatever is needed for the carrying out of the commission. We have not been commissioned to invent the Gospel. That has its origins in God's eternal determination, and its realization in our world through the redemptive work of Christ. The Gospel has been given to us. Our only task is that of spreading it farther, according to our small abilities. It may well be but a small facet of the Gospel's significance that we are able to appropriate in such a manner that we shall be able to give it forth as a living message. Or, to put it more correctly, that is certainly the situation in which we find ourselves. Beyond doubt it is but a fragment of God's rich Gospel that we are able to proclaim. Yet God can through His Spirit bless even that fragment, that His congregation may hear through it exactly that which He wishes to say to them. The Gospel concerning Christ is the Church's true treasure. 'But we have this treasure in earthen vessels, that the infinite power may be God's, and not something which comes from us' (II Cor. 4.7). God's power is mighty in our weakness.

In these pages I have restricted myself almost exclusively to the question of the minister's central task, the bearing forth of the Gospel concerning Christ. For this one great task the manifold duties of the minister have had to remain in the background. Beyond doubt much could have been said about these, and I hope to do so on other occasions. This concentration on the Gospel has brought with it the corollary that I have stressed the joyful and the inspiring aspects of our calling. That does not, however, ignore the fact that the minister's work is by no means easy. On the contrary, many and great are the difficulties which are here encountered, difficulties from within and from without, personal difficulties and difficulties due to the times.

How many a minister has laboured both long and faithfully without being able to see any visible fruit from his labours? For the most part it is of the very nature of our calling that its results can never be objectively computed. When then the pressure of the spirit of the times, alien to the Gospel and indifferent, comes upon one, it is not surprising that many a minister who began his work with glad enthusiasm, after years of apparently fruitless labour becomes faint-hearted and uncertain of his call.

But that is not all. If we look at our task from a more comprehensive perspective, we shall not be able to hide from ourselves the fact that greater difficulties may yet be met. There are many indications that the Church of Christ is moving toward a time when the strain will become more severe than ever, and when there will be demanded of us a contribution of another kind than that to which we are accustomed. In certain parts of the world the Church has received a tangible reminder of the fact that martyrdom does not belong merely to a bygone stage in the history of the Church.

But in the midst of all the external opposition and all the inner uncertainty and weakness which seeks to conquer us, there is one thing which can uphold us and help us over all difficulties—namely, the thought of the great message, the blessed Gospel, which we have been commissioned to preach. That is the seed which is to be sown in all the world. It is indeed true that much will fall by the wayside, upon the stony ground, or among thorns, and become fruitless. But when it falls in good ground, it will bear rich fruit. For the word is not ours, but God's, and in God's word strength dwells. We have only to take care that the word is actually sown, thereafter it is God's concern to give it growth. We are His messengers—that is, we are called by God to be bearers of His message to the world. But, just as it is not we who are to guard the peace of God, but rather God's peace which is to guard us, so also, when all things reel, it is not we who uphold the Gospel, but the Gospel which upholds us. The Gospel gives us the firm ground on which to stand, and the courage we need to carry out our calling. Let us therefore not cast away our courage, but rather hold fast, and let us be borne up by that Gospel which has been entrusted to us.

So shall the peace of God, which surpasses all understanding, guard your hearts and your thoughts, in Christ Jesus.